PENGUIN BOOKS
LILAVATI

Govardhanram Madhavram Tripathi (1855–1907) is best known for his four-volume novel *Sarasvatichandra* (published between 1887–1901). He is also the author of *Snehmudra* (1889), *Navalram Nu Kavijivan* (1891), *The Classical Poets of Gujarat* and *Their Influence on Society and Morals* (1894), *Lilavati Jivankala* (1905), *Dayaram No Aksherdeha* (1908). He presided over the first session of the Gujarati Sahitya Parishad in 1905.

Tridip Suhrud has translated the *Sarasvatichandra* into English. He is Professor and Provost, CEPT University and Director, Lalbhai Dalpatbhai Institute of Indology, Ahmedabad.

LILAVATI

~ A LIFE ~

GOVARDHANRAM
M. TRIPATHI

Translated by

TRIDIP SUHRUD

PENGUIN BOOKS

An imprint of Penguin Random House

PENGUIN BOOKS

USA | Canada | UK | Ireland | Australia
New Zealand | India | South Africa | China

Penguin Books is part of the Penguin Random House group of companies
whose addresses can be found at global.penguinrandomhouse.com

Published by Penguin Random House India Pvt. Ltd
4th Floor, Capital Tower 1, MG Road,
Gurugram 122 002, Haryana, India

Penguin
Random House
India

First published in Gujarati as *Lilavati Jivankala* in 1905
First published in English in Penguin Books by Penguin Random House India 2022

English translation and introduction copyright © Tridip Suhrud 2022

ISBN 9780143444701

Typeset in Adobe Caslon Pro by Manipal Technologies Limited, Manipal
Printed at Thomson Press India Ltd, New Delhi

www.penguin.co.in

In Memory of Ankit Chadha
(1987–2018) and for Megha Todi

Contents

Contents

Translator's Introduction

I

I wish to produce, or see produced, not this or that event—but a people who shall be higher and stronger than they are, who shall be better able to look and manage for themselves than is the present *helpless* generation of my educated and uneducated countrymen. What kind of a nation that should be and how that spark should be kindled for the organic flame: these were, and are, the problems before my mind. I lay

down this as, for the present, the only one fixed
objective before me . . .[1]

With these words Govardhanram Madhavram
Tripathi (1855–1907) articulated his *svadharma*.
Govardhanram was born on 20 October 1855, in
a Vadnagara Nagar Brahmin family at Nadiad.
This Vaishnav family had no remarkable tradition
of learning, and for at least three generations had

---

[1] K. C. Pandya, R. P. Bakshi and S. J. Pandya (eds), *Govardhanram
Madhavram Tripathi's Scrap-Book* (Bombay: N. M. Tripathi,
1959), pp. 29–30, emphasis in the original. The *Scrap-Book* for
the period 1894–1904, edited by the same editors, appeared in
1959. The *Scrap-Book* for the period 1904–06, edited by K. C.
Pandya was published earlier in 1957. Hereafter these volumes
are referred to as *Scrap-Book* I, II and III respectively. Although
the chronology of publication goes against this arrangement,
this has been done for the convenience of citation as well as
to maintain the chronology in which they were written in the
first instance by Govardhanram. Govardhanram began writing
the *Scrap-Book* in January 1885, after he had achieved some
stability in his profession as a lawyer in Bombay. He stopped
maintaining them in November 1906. During this period, he
filled seven notebooks, all of which were written in English.
Govardhanram had no intention of publishing them. They were
published as a part of the celebrations to mark the centenary of
his birth.

practised moneylending. Govardhanram spent his formative years in Bombay and Nadiad. He acquired primary education in the Buddhivardhak Gujarati Shala in Bombay and Government English School at Nadiad. In 1871 Govardhanram passed his matriculation examination as a student of Elphinstone School.

Govardhanram joined the Elphinstone College for his BA degree. Between 1871 and 1875 he studied History, Economics, Nyaya and Nitishastra. He passed his BA examination in the second attempt at the age of twenty.

After passing his BA, Govardhanram made three resolutions which he hoped would govern his entire life. He resolved to acquire a law degree, to start an independent legal practice and to give up legal practice at the age of forty to dedicate the rest of his life to the service of the people through literature.

In 1876 he passed his first LLB examination. He was forced by circumstances to accept the post of a personal secretary to Samaldas Parmanddas, the Dewan of Bhavnagar state. He was repeatedly frustrated in his attempts to pass the LLB examination. He failed three times and eventually passed it in 1883 in the fourth attempt. He immediately left Bhavnagar for Bombay, where at the age of twenty-nine he started his independent legal practice. His practice at the Bombay High Court flourished. At the height of his legal career, he fulfilled his long-cherished dream: at the age of forty-two he retired from the practice to contemplate the state of his people and society in the quiet solitude of his ancestral home in Nadiad.

II

For Govardhanram, the original cause of the universe lies in what he describes as the Great Will or the Great Force. Individual beings are a mere point, a manifestation of the Great Will. 'Our will is a manifestation, at a point, of His will. His will is universal, ours is a point of it.'[2] The vocation of human beings, according to him is to understand the Great Will and function in harmony with it. 'We are unable to enter into the actual motives of the Great Will, but we can understand and join its

---

[2] *Scrap-Book* I, p. 45.

music and poetry . . . Our final cause—like all final causes—is to understand our proper function in this symphony and join it properly.'[3]

A perfect conscience, according to Govardhanram, recognises that 'I is a fiction',[4] and it is at this moment of recognition of self-identity that the individual being is in perfect harmony and union with the Great Will. In this union and realisation of identity lies salvation. But how is this salvation to be attained? The central question for Govardhanram is: how can an individual reconcile his vocation of final union with the Great Force, and his obligation towards his family, the society and the country? For Govardhanram, the final union and duties towards the society can be attained only through what he describes as a 'Philosophy of Consumption'.[5]

Total sacrifice of the individual for the good
of the whole is consumption . . . Complete

---

[3] Ibid., p. 123.

[4] Ibid., p. 46.

[5] The term 'Philosophy of Consumption' is Govardhanram's coinage. In Gujarati he used a term *Uttsargsiddhi*, the attainment of higher ideals through the act of sacrifice.

dissolution and sacrifice of the self for others is consumption. It is through consumption that individual existence and life achieve completion.[6]

Consumption for Govardhanram is an all-encompassing philosophy and praxis. It is by leading a life of consumption that an individual offers his body/soul to the *Yajna* of the Great Force. 'We must consume, both body and soul, . . . in the Great and Patent *Yajna* that is blazing around us, we throw as *Havis* (Oblation) the patent *Yajna* of body and soul . . .'[7]

The philosophy of consumption becomes the sole mediator between the individual and the Great Will and the individual and the society. Consumption of an individual is conditioned by the capacities of the person. 'Consumption . . . is not a promiscuous or unlimited duty. It is actually limited, and potentially unlimited, that it may be enlarged according to capacity.'[8] Notions of morality, ethics and justice

---

[6] Ramprasad P. Bakshi, *Govardhanram Nu Manorajya*, 2nd edition (Bombay: N. M. Tripathi, 1992), pp. 14–15.

[7] *Scrap-Book* I, p. 148.

[8] Ibid., p. 125.

are also contingent upon the idea of consumption. Defining vice and virtue, he wrote:

> Whatever makes a man feed on the flesh of the world, is ordinarily vice. Whatever is his consumption in order to feed the world, is a virtue. Whatever is inconsistent with such consumption and means of attaining of it is vice. Whatever is consistent with it, is innocent. Whatever furthers it is virtue. Whenever feeding oneself is instrumental to such consumption, it is virtue.[9]

A person who recognises virtue and vice, and adopts the former and shuns the latter has a sense of duty. Thus, for Govardhanram, consumption is not only a virtue but it is dharma.

This conception of dharma informed his vocation and defined his understanding of personal duty towards the country.

While clarifying for himself 'duties in regard to the country', Govardhanram set before himself the

---

[9] Ibid., p. 52.

goal of moulding a generation of people who shall be 'higher and stronger' and 'better able to manage for themselves'.

In this articulation of *Svadharma*, Govardhanram is denying the relevance and the efficacy of *events*. Events for him are all acts uninformed by deep industry and knowledge. He also eschewed commenting upon them. Aware as he was of 'the evil consequences which we may inflict on our country by our well-meaning follies', he decided to 'attempt or wish to assist nothing', before proper study. Because 'without study there is no sight and without sight no efficacy of action'.[10] In order to attain the requisite clarity to play out his conflicting, contradictory emotions, desires, feelings and ideas, Govardhanram regularly maintained his personal diaries—the *Scrap-Books*.

Neither the magnitude of the task nor such daunting realisations deviated him from his self-chosen path. 'I must fancy', he says 'that I am an *Ajaramar*, when planning my duty to my country.'[11]

---

[10] *Scrap-Book*, I, pp. 29–30.
[11] Ibid., p. 27. *Ajaramar* means ageless and deathless.

III

It was as a part of his duty towards the country that Govardhanram embarked upon a project which was to consume him for nearly fifteen years. At the age of thirty, in 1885, he started writing his novel *Sarasvatichandra*.[12] When the final part was published in 1901, fourteen years had elapsed between the publication of the first and the fourth and last part. He had not wished to write a novel at all. His initial plan was to write philosophical essays on the human condition. Upon reflection, he found the essay form limiting.

> The conviction has also grown upon him (author) that reality in flesh and blood under the guise of fiction can supply the ordinary reader with subtler moulds and finer casts for

---

[12] All four parts of the novel are available in Tridip Suhrud's English translation. Part 1, *Buddhidhan's Administration* (New Delhi: Orient BlackSwan, 2015), Part 2, *Gunasundari's Household* (New Delhi: Orient BlackSwan, 2016), Part 3, *Ratnanagari's Statecraft* (New Delhi: Orient BlackSwan, 2016), and Part 4, *The Dreamland of Sarasvatichandra and Culmination* (New Delhi: Orient BlackSwan, 2017).

the formation of his inner self, than abstract discussions and that this is especially so with *a people who must be made, and not simply left, to read.*[13]

With the progress of his enterprise, we sense a satisfaction of accomplishment. 'The purpose of the writer is to enable the reader to rise to a stage higher than where he was ... *Sarasvatichandra*, thus undertaken at this point, *works* without doubt, and people *feel* the book. This is a mere literary work and will work on society.'[14]

Eleven years after the publication of the first volume, he notes with satisfaction that 'the progress of the reading classes is equal to the aspirations of the writer to interest them in the principal problems of the day'.[15]

---

[13] Govardhanram Madhavram Tripathi, *Sarasvatichandra*, Part 1 (Bombay: N. M. Tripathi, first published in 1887, eighteenth edition, 1977), English Preface, p. 8. There are two prefaces to the volume, one in Gujarati and the other in English with substantial variation between the two. Emphasis in the original.

[14] *Scrap-Book*, I, p. 31. Emphasis in the original.

[15] *Sarasvatichandra*, part 3, English Preface, p. 3.

The act of writing the novel for Govardhanram is a conscious act of tempering the souls of his countrymen. It is through this act that Govardhanram wishes to fulfil his historical role of an 'organic sheath' between the great civilisational forces and the Indian masses.

IV

The four parts of *Sarasvatichandra* are a reflection on four endeavours of life: politics, household, statecraft and the state of religion, and also on the four ashrams or stages of life: *brahmacharya* (the stage of celibate discipleship), *grihastha* (householder), *vanaprastha* (forest dwelling or detachment from worldly affairs) and *sanyasa* (stage of renunciation). Govardhanram is deeply conscious of the intertwined nature of the fate of his fictional characters and the lives of Lalita and Lilavati (his wife and daughter respectively), especially the character of Gunasundari, who is imagined as an embodiment of the 'domestic angel'. Lilavati is equally conscious of the expectations from her and seeks to live up to the fictional ideal. She, like the other readers of the novel, awaited the resolution of the conflict between widowhood and love in the life of Kumud, the heroine of the novel. In strange ways, her life and the lives of the fictional characters are intertwined. Her initiation into literacy and Govardhanram's literary endeavour commenced almost simultaneously, and she awaited the publication of the final part from her deathbed.

V

Those who came of age in late-nineteenth-century India and felt concerned about the state of their society and nation, had to confront the fact of British presence in India. Awareness of subjection coupled with a profound uncertainty about the present and the future shaped their response to the British presence in India. Given this ultimate objective—'one which never ought to be lost sight of'—of moulding his countrymen and countrywomen into a great people who would be able to take care of themselves, Govardhanram grappled with the meaning of British rule. In an entry in his diary, *Scrap-Book*, dated 13 April 1891, the only unambiguous, unqualified statement was the fact of India's subjection.[16] Accepting the British presence as given, Govardhanram advises his people to cultivate 'elasticity'. 'Coming after offense and defense have been ruled out, "elasticity" becomes the very epitome of ambiguity. The term here seems to suggest pragmatism.'[17] The relations between the rulers and the ruled are mediated by the idea of warfare. But this is not an offensive nor a confrontation. The concept of 'constitutional'—a concept given by the colonial rulers—and the need to cultivate elasticity, introduce an element of caution, of pragmatic moderation.

From there Govardhanram moves on to a depiction of rulers. They are 'clever', 'selfish aggressors' and 'disinterested' yet 'benevolent helpmates'. Here again, Govardhanram displays ambiguous feelings and a mixed assessment of British presence. Yet he is aware that in the ultimate analysis, the coloniser's interests carry the day and

---

[16] *Scrap-Book*, I, p. 51.

[17] Sudhir Chandra, *The Oppressive Present: Literature and Social Consciousness in Colonial India* (New Delhi: Oxford University Press, 1992), p. 23.

whatever ground is gained by Indians through their elasticity is suddenly snatched away.

Govardhanram might have been ambivalent towards the impact of British presence, but he displays remarkable consistency in his analysis of 'native states' and the inability of his people to effectively counter the colonial aggressor. This severe denouncement and total lack of confidence in his countrymen inspired him to mould a generation which shall be 'better able to look and manage for themselves.'

This negative assessment of his countrymen to manage the political and social implications of the colonial encounter pervades all his reflections— in the *Scrap-Books* as well as the novel. He not only emphasises his lack of faith in the strategies employed by Indians to get rid of the British but also questions the basic premise of 'foreign' and 'native' interests being mutually exclusive. Moreover, his lack of trust in the abilities of natives to manage heterogenous people with differing aspirations and needs also colours his assessment of the problem.

He goes on to articulate the real problem: '(The) problem is not the absolute eviction of the foreigner, but *his accommodation to the native element* . . . where India and England *become one on Indian Soil*.'[18] One can assume that while cautioning against attempts to evict the foreigner completely from Indian soil Govardhanram is referring not just to the physical presence, but to a civilisational encounter, and his stand was informed by the awareness that Indian culture and society will be transformed by this 'drama of transition'. The source of his anxiety lay in the uncertainty about the future and how these opposing tendencies would be harmonised and what kind of resolution would emerge. To bring about a resolution where 'England become one on Indian Soil', he thought it was necessary to 'create a homogeneous nuclear class'.

This also was the central concern of *Sarasvatichandra*. At the same time, he was not unaware of the opposition of *foreign* and native interests. He knew that the ruler, however enlightened, would not allow the development of a class of natives who could think of and act for the welfare of the country.

---

[18] Ibid., p. 150.

VI

Govardhanram is a very unnerving cultural possibility. As a cultural possibility he is not our past, but he could potentially be our present. We made a cultural choice that he and *Sarasvatichandra* would not be the marker of the contemporary Gujarati mind.

Sarasvatichandra was written at the founding moment of the Indian National Congress. We shall discuss the political imagination that informs the novel later. Around the same time, another important cultural invention was taking root—the stock market. It represents the fundamental idea of speculation. Speculation not with ideas, philosophies or cultural trajectories but commodities and money.

Both the novel *Sarasvatichandra* and the eponymous hero represent a relationship with money and wealth that is completely contrary to the speculative tendencies represented by the stock market. The novel is sensitive to the possibilities of the stock market and the joint-stock company as creators of wealth and enterprise. But it seeks to valorise not the acquisition but the abdication of wealth. Giving up wealth and cultivating an attitude of trusteeship towards wealth is an unnerving cultural possibility in a mercantile culture, something that M.K. Gandhi was to discover within three decades of the publication of *Sarasvatichandra*. One's cultural unease with Gujarat could begin with one's attitude towards wealth and acquisition.

The reasons for our unease with *Sarasvatichandra* and Govardhanram are perhaps deeper; even deeper than our relationship with wealth. The fundamental idea of Govardhanram—as also of Gandhi later—is that any social, political, ideological change has to begin with the self; it is located in the person and the person quite often extends beyond the self to encompass one's immediate family. In the case of Govardhanram, it encompassed his wife Lalita and their daughter Lilavati. In the case of Gandhi, it included Kastur, Harilal, the ashramic community and us as well. Govardhanram called this the Philosophy of Consumption. Consumption, in its old, original sense, means 'to be consumed'. Complete self-sacrifice lies at the heart of the philosophy of consumption, and Govardhanram's characters aspire to become its embodiment. The author is, of course, not as demanding as Gandhi, but Govardhanram's commitment to the idea is no less for that reason. The demands that he made of middle-class Gujarati culture are very discomfiting. What he demands is total surrender, consumption to the extent that a life is offered as oblation; in his case, two other lives are offered as oblation. *Sarasvatichandra*, unlike anything that was written after it, presents a total system—not a totalitarian system but a total system. It is an endeavour that seeks to encompass everything of the human life in it. It has reflections on the state of polity, on the state of society and the household, on the newly emerging and potentially very disruptive idea of the couple, on the nature of political ideology and a culture that sought to find place in the present for India's past as also contemporary Europe. It also reflects on our relationship with the divine, both as the Maker and as that which signifies rectitude, right action, duty and dharma. This kind of total vision, a vision that is rooted in sacrifice, detachment, right action and common good could be frightening as a socio-cultural possibility.

VII

We are not concerned with the fate of his societal endeavours, but with the fate of Govardhanram and two other individuals irrevocably bound to him. Their minds and souls were the first that he tried to cultivate in accordance with his ideals and philosophy. These two were Lalita, Govardhanram's second wife, and Lilavati, their daughter.

It is important for us to consider the fates of these three not only because they were played out almost simultaneously with his public endeavour, but also because for Govardhanram there was no marked disjunction between giving his country a vision of an ideal society and of educating and 'raising' his wife and daughter. These two projects were essentially the same; both were integral to his personal dharma towards the country. And as Govardhanram himself put it, 'My country is a term which must be confined in the beginning and made to expand in course of time only.'[19]

---

[19] *Scrap-Book*, I, p. 51.

Govardhanram showed keen awareness of the intertwined fates of those inhabiting the inner world that he created through his fiction, and his own self and family. At many places in the *Scrap-Book* he drew parallels between his life and the novel, compared his wife to his heroine and asked his daughter to follow in the footsteps of Gunasundari. His life and his fiction seemed to him to mirror each other. One of his other daughters, Jayanti, was betrothed at a tender age and this decision hurt Govardhanram. Two days after the engagement he wrote, 'Curious coincidence! Jayanti betrothed on 25th, and I get the first proof of the second part of my novel on the 26th. The betrothal pinches me, and I compare myself to Vidya Chatura, who accepting in haste a woman's arguments, betrothed Kumud to Pramad, and dropped all talk of *Sarasvatichandra*.'[20]

In a moment of rare passion Govardhanram had said, '*I only want their souls*.'[21] Moreover, the only source of deriving some understanding about the

---

[20] *Scrap-Book*, I, p. 93. Kumud and Pramad are key characters in *Sarasvatichandra*.

[21] Ibid., p. 27, emphasis in the original.

possible fates of his societal endeavour is the lives of Govardhanram, Lilavati and Lalita, as they tried to live a life of consumptive virtue. It is in their biographies that Govardhanram's 'grand project' unfolds itself completely.

Govardhanram's marriage to Harilaxmi was fixed before their birth. A close 'conjugal' relationship developed between the two but the marriage ended tragically—Harilaxmi died in 1874 while giving birth to their child, who also died soon after. Govardhanram was to express his deep anguish and a sense of permanent loss in two verses, *Hridayruditshatakam* and *Snehmudra*, that he wrote in memory of Harilaxmi and in which he paid glowing tributes to her.[22] Govardhanram was married to Lalitagauri in 1876.[23] He was twenty-one at the time and Lalita was around fifteen or sixteen years of age. Govardhanram, secure in his faith in the Philosophy of Consumption, tried to cultivate in his wife the high ideals of this philosophy. 'My

[22] *Hridayruditshatakam*, a long verse in Sanskrit was written in 1875. *Snehmudra*, which is an adaption of the former, was published in 1889.

[23] Ibid., pp. 167–168.

duty does not end with satisfying her poor ideals, but I am bound to enlarge them. This is my marital duty.'[24] Govardhanram lists his 'duties' towards his wife as follows:

> a) to train her up, b) to raise her life, c) to make her free, d) to provide for her, e) to fulfill her aspirations with such luxuries etc., as a husband in love and duty ought to give her.[25]

For Lalita, the first thirteen years of her life with Govardhanram were years of training under his constant guidance and close supervision. Not given to impassioned displays of his feelings, Govardhanram was nevertheless ecstatic in his praise of Lalita's moral strength to continuously lead a life of self-negation and self-inflicted deprivation. There are repeated references to Lalita's moral virtues and a life of self-sacrifice in his *Scrap-Books* of this period. Govardhanram could not hide his feelings of a personal success and achievement in training

---

[24] Ibid., p. 64.
[25] Ibid., p. 61.

Lalita. 'I have trained wife from the beginning to do voluntary and loving service and sacrifice to my people. She has done it. She has worked like an ass for my people.'[26] Lalita's sole aspiration in life became making Govardhanram and his family happy. For this she earned Govardhanram's unqualified praise. Her latest change of disposition compelled Govardhanram 'to adore and make *arti* to her soul—to her goodness, to her virtue, to her understanding and to her moral power'.[27] Lalita's sacrifice compelled Govardhanram, who constantly lived with a feeling of his own moral and intellectual superiority, to put her on a pedestal even higher than himself. 'Her life is higher than mine.'[28] This was the greatest recognition that Govardhanram could have given to any one, he even called her 'Family's Angel'.[29] Lalita also succeeded in acquiring respect from her quarrelsome and dominating mother-in-law Shivkashi. She compared Lalita to Gunasundari, the ideal and perfect embodiment of

[26] Ibid., pp. 184–185.
[27] Ibid., p. 26.
[28] Ibid.
[29] Ibid.

consumption created by Govardhanram in his novel *Sarasvatichandra*.[30]

However, his 'heaven' does not last for long. Govardhanram recorded instances of conflict between his wife and mother and between Lalita and his brother's wife. He recorded, with some satisfaction, his own efforts to be an 'impartial judge' in these conflicts and reflected on 'family misunderstandings and the way to remove them'.[31] As the conflicts and discord became deeper, he was forced to re-evaluate Lalita's morals and virtues. He was ruthless in condemning her; he writes, 'My wife is inadequate to be my heroine, alas, she falls far too short of my Gunsundari.'[32] Lalita's failure to continuously lead a life of consumption forced Govardhanram to grapple with a more fundamental question of how to successfully 'raise' our women. He also reflects on his own failure to do so. 'Are our women to be raised? How? Take a particular woman, and see, how? . . . I have tried them with

---

[30] Ibid.

[31] Ibid., pp.113–115.

[32] Ibid., p. 200.

my mother, my wife . . . The result of my labours have been that both mother and wife have turned into discontented imperfect machines—square pegs in round holes—my mother the peg and my wife the hole!'[33] Even this clear admission of failure did not introduce any element of doubt regarding his mission of cultivating minds and tempering the souls of his countrymen. Instead, quite characteristically, he saw in this failure a new raison d'être' for his endeavours: '99 out of 100 individuals will give up without thinking of the society', he says, but, 'my crucifixion in my own family must direct me to raise from this grave and try to relieve my countrymen from the troubles from which I could not relieve myself. *The next generation must always benefit by the adversities of its predecessors.*'[34]

Govardhanram was unwavering in his resolve to cultivate the minds of others, but by 1892 Lalita was no longer prepared to lead a life of continuous self-negation. Lalita became the victim of many physical and mental ailments. 'Mrs. has been suffering from

---

[33] Ibid., pp. 236–237.
[34] Ibid. Emphasis added.

premonitory symptoms of consumption . . . she is doomed.'[35] As her physical condition further deteriorated, her mental health also suffered. She became a patient of 'Monomania' and was admitted to a sanatorium at Sion.[36]

Despite care and medical treatment, her condition progressively worsened, and she was faced with imminent death. 'Poor Lalita! Your life is hanging upon a most apparent uncertainty. Most people affected as you are, die after lingering pains.'[37] The possibility of Lalita's death compelled Govardhanram to articulate his own guilt: 'Poor beloved Lalita, sweet sharer of my cares, brave bearer of the heavy burdens that I have placed on thy frail personality, in this way am I bound to witness thy pangs and smoldering . . .'[38]

Lalita survived. But, after this point Govardhanram gave up his efforts to cultivate Lalita.

---

[35] Ibid., p. 162.
[36] Ibid., pp. 166–168.
[37] Ibid., p. 166.
[38] Ibid., pp. 163–164.

VIII

In 1881 Lalita gave birth to their first child—daughter Lilavati. In 1885 Govardhanram started writing *Sarasvatichandra*, at the same time when Lilavati's education began. Govardhanram assumed total control of her education and upbringing.

In Govardhanram's project neither chance nor *lila* (play of the divine) had any play. Each action was to be based on proper study and intense reflection. This 'obsessive concern for clarity' is also reflected in the detailed curriculum that he worked out for Lilavati's education.

Lilavati was admitted to a girl's school in Zaver Baug (Bombay) at the age of three. Govardhanram soon realised the narrow vision of such institutions and its futility in Lilavati's education. She was taken out of the school after a few months. She was never to go to a school after this. This brief stay at a girls' school was to be her only excursion to the world outside before her marriage without the ever-present gaze of her father.

Govardhanram wanted Lilavati to have comprehensive training appropriate for a young woman of her social background destined to marry. This he felt could be best achieved by a training in Sanskrit, Gujarati and English, both as languages and as types of knowledge that would become available through that language. In the biography he gives a detailed account of the books that she was taught, given to read and her responses to them as also the reasons why she was allowed not to pursue English education beyond the primary readers, and the measures that were taken to ameliorate this particular lack.

Govardhanram was seized by a sense of urgency about Lilavati's education, which was comprehensive. No area was left untouched. So complete was Govardhanram's involvement with Lilavati that he neglected his two other daughters, Jayanti and Jasu, and also son Ramaniyaram's education and upbringing. In the later years, he often used to lament the fact that in his own preoccupation with his literary and professional activities and total involvement with Lilavati he had neglected his other children, including the son. Govardhanram notes that even Lilavati had noticed the wide gulf which separated her from her brother and sisters. She even questioned Govardhanram on this and his meek defense left her unsatisfied.[39]

Lilavati was engaged to marry at the age of three or four. While choosing a husband for her, Govardhanram went against the established norm of his caste of choosing a family from his own native town Nadiad. She was engaged to Himmatbhai, the third son of Manilal Gangashankar of Petlad. Govardhanram's family was against Lilavati's betrothal to an impoverished and indebted family. But, Govardhanram was uncompromising and argued that even his own family was indebted at the time of his marriage to Lalita but her parents reposed complete faith in their ability to overcome the crisis. He argued that they had no right to reject Himmatbhai's family on grounds of indebtedness.

---

[39] Ibid., p. 50. One incident captures this divide. Once while he was going to Bombay from Nadiad, Jayanti requested him to get for her a book on religious and ritual observances, *Somvar Ni Katha*. After she left the room, Govardhanram expressed his deep pain and his sense of failure to his friend and relative Chandrashankar Pandya. 'I could not educate this poor girl and therefore she has to ask for books like *Somvar Ni Katha*, otherwise like Lilavati she would have demanded excellent books.' *Sriyut Govardhanram*, pp. 207–208.

Lilavati's wedding to Himmatbhai took place in 1891, when she was twelve years old. Her marriage at this tender age irked Govardhanram. But he finally decided to go ahead with it. He reasoned that her happiness had to be sought within the existing social structure and this marriage was necessary to achieve that.[40]

The process of her education continued even after she was sent to live with her in-laws. Both Govardhanram and Lalita wrote frequent letters to her, in which they counselled her in *Grihini Dharma*, or the duties of a householder. Father Govardhanram urged her to follow the ideal and noble path of Gunasundari.

Lilavati made this philosophy of life integral to her existence. She followed each tenet as truth itself. Govardhanram lists many examples—and not without great satisfaction and some degree of pride—to prove that Lilavati had been worthy of all the knowledge that he had given her and that she had internalised completely this knowledge and the principles of consumption.

---

[40] *Scrap-Book*, I, p. 89.

Govardhanram notes many instances to reinforce that she lived her life in accordance with the two basic tenets of the Philosophy of Consumption: *Yajmandharma* and *Manojnadharma*.[41]

Govardhanram's success in creating an embodiment of the principles of consumptive virtue through Lilavati was complete.

Lilavati lived in Junagadh, which suffered a series of epidemics. Her parents repeatedly asked her to join them in Nadiad. But Lilavati refused to leave her in-law's house till she had nursed every member of the family. When Lilavati finally reached Nadiad, it was too late. She had 'consumed' herself through self-inflicted privation. She was diagnosed as suffering from the disease of 'consumption',

---

[41] Govardhanram defined virtue as consumption of self in order to feed the world, while vice was feeding on the flesh of the world. The dharma of the virtuous is to be a *Yajaman* while those who feed on the others are *atithi*. He imagined the ideal character as the follower of *Yajamandharma*. The other quality of the virtuous is to understand even the unarticulated feelings and desires of others and conduct their lives accordingly. He calls this *Manojnadharma*. He had attributed these qualities to the *sadhvis* of Sundargiri in *Sarasvatichandra*.

tuberculosis. She refused to blame any person or even her fate in the face of imminent death.

Lilavati died at the age of twenty-one, on 8 January 1902. It is perhaps not a coincidence that two projects which had taken complete hold of Govardhanram's being ended almost simultaneously. He completed the fourth and final part of his novel *Sarasvatichandra* a short while earlier, and it was published in 1901.

Govardhanram performed one final act of his duty towards the sacred memory of Lilavati and his country. He wrote her biography, *Lilavati Jivankala*. Even this final act was undertaken not to glorify her memory but to place before society the story of an ideal life.

IX

Lilavati Jivankala is a forgotten text in contemporary Gujarat. Between 1905, when it was first published, and 1961 the book was reprinted four times. Despite its attraction for readers, only one substantial reflection on the book and its relationship to Govardhanram's other writings exists till date in

Guajarati. This is by the poet and critic Balwantrai K. Thaokre (1869–1952) based on two lectures that he gave in 1913 and 1920–1921. The possible reasons for this critical indifference to *Lilavati Jivankala* are difficult to gauge. Till today it remains perhaps the only biography or life story of a daughter written by her father in the late 19th century and early 20th century, not only in Gujarati but perhaps in Indian bhasha writings. Gujarati does not have any other example of its kind except a few elegiac poems by poet fathers for their departed sons. *Lilavati Jivankala* bears all the marks of Govardhanram's Gujarati prose; it is dense, almost opaque at some places, with heavy reliance upon words with their roots in Sanskrit and is interspersed with Sanskrit verses.

The reason for the indifference probably lies in the very basis of this life story and the trajectory of that idea in Gujarat/Gujarati. The Philosophy of Consumption, the idea that one needs to consume oneself in the service of others, primarily the country, received a large cultural endorsement from Gandhi. Gandhi called this by another name, *Yajna*. The cultural and economic trajectory of modern Gujarat in the post-Independence period has rendered both Philosophy of Consumption and *Yajna* as irrelevant. It is a society that aspires for greater acquisition, accumulation and consumption.

X

Who or what was responsible for Lilavati's tragic and untimely death? Father Govardhanram, who assumed complete control of her life and tried to create a real embodiment of his philosophy? Can he be held responsible? Or was it his philosophy, which demanded negation of the 'self', that was responsible? Or should we hold Lilavati's husband and his parents responsible? Or was it the will of the Great Will? *Lilavati Jivankala* does not provide any answers.

We must turn to Govardhanram's *Scrap-Books* to understand his emotions. Initially, Govardhanram is tempted to attribute her pain and suffering to the desire of the Great Will. 'My best, sweetest, meekest, wisest and most patient child, who has done nothing in this life to deserve this situation, a situation which can only be accounted for by a speculative desire of Providence to kill her, or to test or toughen the "Philosophy" of which alone her education and wealth consists.'[42]

This attribution to the Great Will was only temporary. He feels that neither Lilavati's husband nor the parents-in-law deserved to have a noble soul like Lilavati in their house. The restrained emotions expressed in *Lilavati Jivankala* find a free expression in his *Scrap-Book*, where there are repeated references to the ill treatment, agony and prolonged suffering that she was subjected to by her parents-in-law.

Her services were not only accepted without the slightest effort at limiting her struggle to serve them, but she was taunted for her groans and complaints, which she could not have made except in extremities. Her complaints were belittled, she was allowed to pass latest hours of a coldest winter on a damp ground floor, working to do them superfluous service without being relieved. And when she had fever and

---

[42] *Scrap-Book*, II, 191.

shiverings and was in need of warm blankets to cover her, nobody looked to these things. She lay so, listening to talks with hard words about her making too much of her body.'[43]

He does not see any escape from this situation. If she were to live, she would have to go back to her husband. Only death could save her from this misery. He secretly desires her death.

Not being able to see how the girl can be happy by living with such people as those at her husband's, I have never been able to persuade myself to offer a single prayer for her life, and all that I could do in my affection, which cannot bear the idea of her death, has been to request the Great Will to do what is best for her welfare, and for his inscrutable objects, or to make her live *provided* she is destined to be happy by living.[44]

---

[43] Ibid., p. 224.
[44] Ibid., p. 213. Emphasis in the original.

Blaming others might have given temporary solace to Govardhanram the father but the thinker in him is not convinced. He knows that the final decision regarding Lilavati's marriage was his and he had gone against both the norms of his community and the express wishes of his family while taking this decision. He gives a long, agonising justification for his action.[45] Such post-facto wisdom does not lessen his burden. His search for the truth finally leads him to the realisation: 'I am responsible.'[46] The realisation invokes in him a strong feeling of having sinned. 'I have to thank myself for my having committed this inexplicable sin against my poor child, by choosing for her an unsuitable family.'[47] With her death, his feeling of having committed a sin takes hold of him.

> At 5.30 p.m. yesterday my poor Lilavati died after a stainless, spotless life of suffering. She was a martyr to the cause of our Hindu Social

---

[45] Ibid., p. 223.
[46] Ibid., p. 191.
[47] Ibid., p. 216.

System, to her father's exercise of his power of disposing of her in early marriage with reform modification and to the services she rendered to her mother-in-law and her father-in-law.[48]

Now his expiation and atonement can lie only in 'realising my faults and weakness, and my sins against her life and merits'.[49] He also concludes that 'her soul and holiness were superior to *mine* and to that of every other person I see about me.'[50] Only one idea gives him solace: 'I can only feel proud to have had a child like this during my worldly sojourn, rewarded at the idea that I had the privilege of looking after the education and elevation of so aspiring a soul.'[51] His search for atonement leads him to examine the education and 'elevation' of her soul. 'In Lilavati's life, I and her mother always taught her the way to do her duty to her husband and his family, and to seek reward and consolation

---

[48] Ibid., p. 220.

[49] Ibid., p. 228.

[50] Ibid. Emphasis in the original.

[51] Ibid., p. 228.

in the idea of Duty. She was quite equal to her task and her body paid for it.'[52] He continues,

> and with the philosophy and sweetness that her education and innate powers were able to develop in her, her life became one of martyrdom, among other things, to her own very high sense of duty, in which point she out-distanced not only me and mine but all the characters that I have been able to spin out in my books.[53]

In the opening lines of *Sanskarkala-Shodashi*, a long poem on Lilavati, Govardhanram laments:

> I had conceived a Gunsundari in my head. In real life I fathered you, a better version of Gunsundari. You did penance like Gunsundari but unlike her, did not enjoy the fruit thereof. I produced a thesis, you sacrificed your life to prove it right![54]

---

[52] Ibid., p. 224.

[53] Govardhanram to Janmanshankar Buch, Appendix XIII, p. 241.

[54] *Sanskar–Shodashi*, published in *Lilavati Jivankala*, pp. 133–155. The verse has been translated by Sonal Shukla. 'Govardhanram's

Having realised that it was his education, his philosophy which was the real reason for Lilavati's pain, suffering and death, Govardhanram is forced to re-evaluate his project of cultivation of minds and elevation of souls.

> My daughter Lilavati suffered because of high virtues and would have fared better if she had not got the virtues! Is it right then to teach these virtues to our daughters? So many people tell my wife that she has killed Lilavati by making her virtuous, the charge comes home more to me. Is a parent right in educating his children in this way at their cost?'[55]

He questions the idea of virtue itself. But he is not ready to give up either his project or his faith in the essential goodness of virtue. He, for the final time, reasserts the validity of the principles of consumption: 'This question must be answered in *affirmative* for people like *myself*; my children,

---

Women', *EPW*, 31 October 1987. P. WS-65.
[55] *Scrap-Book*, II, pp. 290–291.

like their father and mother, have been educated in virtues *irrespective of its consequences.*'[56]

The power of his vision did not allow Govardhanram to abandon his project but, with Lilavati's death, the creative self of Govardhanram died. He lived his final years lonely and miserable, seeking solace and strength form Lilavati's memory.

No misery that will reach me now can be higher or more excruciating than that borne by my Lilavati, and I can do no better reverence to her sacred memory than by walking in her gentle and yet, firm, steady, virtuous, and heroic footsteps in facing any circumstances that may befall me. Her sweet and lofty virtues be my divine beacon-light in my mundane struggles henceforth! May her example inspire my soul and draw me closer unto hers wherever and whatsoever she now may be![57]

He died on 4 January 1907 after a long illness.

---

[56] Ibid., emphasis in the original.

[57] *Scrap-Book*, II, p. 256.

XI

Govardhanram was convinced about both the necessity and desirability of his vision, of his striving and his authority to demand such strivings from 'his' women—Lalita and Lilavati in his life and Gunasundari and Kumud in his fiction. It is apparent that he wanted change but with one constant. He demanded and obtained sacrifice from and of women. Gunasundari paid for his vision through consumption and Kumud by submitting her desires to a higher ideal of ascetic renunciation. When his real-life 'domestic angel', Lalita, became hysterical under his regimentation and gathered the courage to question his ideals, he made another attempt through Lilavati. Lilavati paid with her life. Govardhanram, while striving to forge a people who were higher and stronger, was also bound to his times and his own convictions. The readers of Lilavati's life would not remain untouched by the deep ambivalence and contradictions that Govardhanram harboured within him and in his writing. It is this deep cleavage that finally weighed on his creativity after the death of Lilavati.

Lilavati Jivankala is an unsettling text, even for the present translator who has deep engagement with the life of Harilal Gandhi.[58] The reason why Lilavati and Harilal have attracted me is not for their pathos but because they are grand cautionary tales. Both the fathers in their light sought to mould a daughter and a son. The son rebelled (and when Harilal left home for the first time, Gandhi remarked that this was the influence of reading Govardhanram's *Sarasvatichandra*) and the daughter sought to obey. Both the rebellion and the obedience created a tragic life. It is perhaps not surprising that both Lilavati and Harilal died of consumption, tuberculosis.

Tridip Suhrud

---

[58] See, C.B. Dalal, *Harilal Gandhi: A Life*, translated with an introduction by Tridip Suhrud (Chennai: Orient BlackSwan, 2007).

Lilavati Jivankala

Author's Preface

Lilavati was the eldest daughter of the author. This book has been written by her proud father. It has been divided in three parts: The first part is a prose biography of Lilavati. The second part contains a poem 'Sanskar Sodashi'. The third part is a poem 'Parlok'.[1] The second and third parts are also addressed to Lilavati. A father can but only partially and incompletely collect the events in the life of his daughter. The biography is marked by

---

[1] The present translation does not include the two poetic compositions.

this incompleteness. But not just that, only these aspects of her life which were considered worth of being enshrined in the hearts of the people have been included here. The second part contains the essence that has emerged from this churning. The first two parts essentially deal with this worldly life of Lilavati. The third part is an attempt to bring into the mind's eye her other-worldly life.

Nadiad
G.M.T.
Ashvin Samvat: 1961

1

The Sources of Lilavati's Life

Lilavati aged 8 or 9

One day, Lilavati stopped playing her game, came to me and asked, 'Mota Kaka,[2] what is in our stomach?' I explained to her something about the intestine and the process by which food enters it and the way it is absorbed. She heard me intently, deep in thoughts, and then ran away. Soon, thereafter,

---

[2] Lilavati addressed her father Govardhanram as Mota Kaka, literally elder uncle, this rather unusual form of address may have originated from her cousins addressing Govardhanram as 'Mota Kaka.'

her mother came and asked, 'What did you explain to Moti, the elder one? She's saying, "Ba, our being Nagar Brahmin is all false!"' Lilavati began to explain, 'Mota Kaka, did I say anything wrong? All this bathing and cleansing is only external, isn't it? The stomach is filled with dirt and stale food! All the bathing that the Nagar Brahmins do is only external, but internal cleansing is something else.'

Behn, we saw during your ever-so-brief life the seeds of this wisdom grow into a tree.

Lilavati's aged 10 or 11

'Mota Kaka, what is the reason for marriage? Cannot people be allowed to not marry and remain single?' One day, very subtly, Lilavati posed this question. The question set me thinking. When Lilavati was two years old, and we lived in Bhavnagar, I would take her in my lap and sing to her *Snehmudra*, which was being composed at that time, in order to put her to sleep. In that poem, a Hindu daughter asks a similar question to her learned father. Did Lilavati's conscience imbued with the poem pose similar questions to me? What fate awaits her in marriage?

In this country and in my caste, it is my duty to determine that part of her destiny and, as her duty, it would fall upon Lilavati to accept that fate. In another country she would not have the occasion to ask this question. Before these thoughts found a stop, Lilavati posed the question again and stood somewhat abashed before me. What am I to say to this child? As my anxiety grew, her eagerness also increased. Eventually, a response had to be given. I drew her closer to me and caressed her back and replied, 'Behn, you have been born in this family and our customs are a part of our lives and, therefore, you cannot but be married. Mothers and fathers do not live forever and so, in their absence, the daughters need some protection.' She said nothing and went away, apparently satisfied.

A blessing arose in my heart. 'Behn, I too am one of our people and this life of a householder has been a fulfilling one for me, and that is all by the grace of God. May you receive similar blessings from Him.' These were the benedictions of a human heart. How many hearts offer such blessings? It would be appropriate to say that all those who have daughters utter such blessings. Our scriptures in a myriad form seek to explain how happiness and sorrow are distributed and what laws govern such distribution. The efficacy of such blessings also follow these laws.

Lilavati! Today I am able to see the effect of my blessings on your heart. Before you posed the question, long before you were born, a father—born of my imagination—was asked a similar question by his daughter, also born of my imagination. The daughter commented on the wedding fixed for her by her father:

> *Daughter of a scholar father,*
> *I studied under his tutelage. My mind broadened*
> *and heart pined for virtues.*
> *A child, I cherished many aspirations.*
> *But O', I didn't know the destiny writ for a Hindu.*
> *Child myself, my hand was given to an unknown*
> *child. I*
> *was signed off to purgatory by my teacher and elder.*[3]

The daughter of my imaginations, who desired happiness and pleasure, uttered words of dejection

---

[3] *Snehmudra* (Verses 10–12).

and dissatisfaction. But the profound concern that your father had for your welfare found a place in the deep recesses of your heart. The essence of your life, your unsaid words and your actions have always indicated your satisfaction with these efforts and it has been my experience and it has come to me as an object lesson that you desired not joys and pleasures but a life of duty, penance and dedication to your husband. No other desire has taken root within you, nor have they ever sprouted. This was the unsaid benediction of my heart and its effect was evident in the core of your being and through your actions. But this could also be said in praise of you; considering our relationship in this world, I cannot say that I am not partial to you and that a father cannot see anything but virtues of his daughter. But it is what it is. I do not write this in praise of you. I am moved by a conviction that the essence of your life and your words have a lesson for our society. You are the real author of this book. Moreover, after your death, many daughters like you have been born to many parents, they are alive and shall stay so. I can see how your essence permeates their soul. And I consider all of them Lilavati. Hence, dear reader, in this book, the name 'Lilavati' addresses many others. Consider that these words of mine are addressed to all those who are Lilavati, and that Lilavati is the real author of this work and it is through her father—bound in duty and religion—that she speaks to other Lilavatis.

1

There's a deep sense of satisfaction that follows the act of *kanyadan*, and the acceptance of this gift in marriage, customarily expressed at the end of the wedding ceremony. And yet, when the moment arrives for the girl to depart from her marital home, her parents' hearts ache and eyes cry out in agony. This cry of agony is the first sign of concern about the fate that awaits their daughter. This is the beginning of the deep and abiding apprehension which requires years of patience and observation to finally ascertain the conduct of her husband and his family that truly secures their daughter's position in their home. Until then, the anxiety and concern do not come to an end.

Lilavati, by posing the aforementioned question before her marriage, made me experience that anxiety once, and then again I was made to experience it at the end of her nuptial ceremony. From the time she reached her in-laws' house, she made attempts to assuage this anxiety and her endeavour continued till her death.

This anxiety, which began with her question, was attempted to put to rest as soon as she set her foot at her in-laws' house. In the middle of 1895, I was in Porbandar for some work. Lilavati was in Petlad, at her in-laws'. Some rumour regarding her condition worried me and I wrote to her from Porbandar, asking after her health and other matters. In response, she wrote:

I had fever for a day in Nadiad, and for one more day in Petlad, but I am better now. You have written in *Snehmudra*:

Leaving the egg, bird takes a new life,
Leaves the parent having learnt to feed and fly.

Similarly, I know the last verse of the fourth act of *Shakuntal*. Do write to me about your rheumatism. Kindly do not be anxious and worry about me. God will do good by me.

She was fourteen when she said this. When this author gave the responsibility of her education to Shastriji Jivram,[4] he had outlined the purpose of her education thus:

> Shastriji, Lilavati is destined to live in a foreign environment. Neither I nor her mother will be able to guide her in good and bad times. Moreover, who are we—worldly beings—to provide her with wisdom? So, if you impart knowledge to her, offer the kind of knowledge that will be a loyal friend to her intellect and constantly guide her, wherever she may be, on the right path.

Shastriji did us the kindness of granting our request and Lilavati fulfilled her role with her efforts and drew the author's attention to the last verse of *Shakuntal*. In this verse, having sent Shakuntala to her husband's house, her father says:

---

[4] Shastri Jivram Lallubhai, later a professor of Sanskrit, Elphinstone College, Bombay.

A girl is held in trust, another's treasure;
To arms of love my child to-day is given;
And now I feel a calm and sacred pleasure
I have restored the pledge that came from heaven.[5]

Obeying our custom of not uttering the name of the husband before elders, not only did Lilavati mention only the number of the verse, but she also did not write the verse with terms such as 'arms of love'. She gave her concerned father the example of Kanva Rishi and counselled, 'You have performed the duty enjoined upon you and now it is improper for you to be concerned about me.' She had studied the Gita and she invoked the lesson of 'Let right deeds be thy motive, and not fruits that come from that.'[6] She suggested that the bonds of the body and other worldly relations are fleeting and their dissolution does not merit either attachment or sorrow. The bond shared between a father and a daughter is destined by the Great Will and she reminded me of

---

[5] Kalidasa, *Translation of Shakuntala and other works*, by Arthur William Ryder (London: J.M. Dent and Co., 1912) p. 50.

[6] Discourse II: verse 47.

13

this by quoting the lines from my own poem. Dear Lilavati, you made me realise that you had acquired the right and the capacity to invoke the essence and cadence of the verse of the Mahakavi Kalidasa, and, having understood its meaning, you exercised your authority to counsel me. Lilavati, if I do not accept your authority, then who will? And I have, as a sign of acceptance of your authority, preserved your letter, which I publish today. Or no—maybe not—it is probably you, an immortal presence in my heart, causing this to be published so that all fathers can learn from it. In your letter, you did not mention the cause of your fever; instead you wrote, 'Kindly do not be anxious and worry about me. God will do good by me.' You even asked me about my rheumatism. I am not to worry about you, but you shall inquire about my well-being! Lilavati . . . such love! Such sense of duty and wisdom emanated from your heart all your life and manifested in your actions. There is a saying that it is possible for a progeny to deviate from their duty (they are seen as *kaputa*) but never is there a mother who does not perform her duty (*kartavya*). Whereas, in our household, it so happened that in counselling and educating you, our hearts became harsh and bereft of emotion but, in receiving those lessons, your heart remained ever tender and affectionate towards us.

2

Which part of our advice and counselling was so hard and harsh? We wrote many letters to you and so did you, but all those letters could not be preserved. But as God willed, your first letter quoted above and the very last letter that you wrote are with me. What did we find from your possession after your death? The letters which were mundane and worldly were not found but those which contained advice and which sought to guide you were found among your possessions. To illustrate what was dear and close to your heart, I cite two examples. These were what you preserved as wealth in an otherwise impoverished life.

At the very beginning of your married life, at your in-laws', your mother wrote to you:

Parents-in-law occupy the place of parents, *Jeth–Jethani* are akin to your brother and sister-in-

15

law. Therefore, you must consider them as your own and in your conduct you should have equal affection for all. So long as you have the feelings of distance and separation, your mind shall not experience joy. Therefore, you must consider them as your own and it is your duty to not cause them any pain and considering them equal to gods. You had once asked me who is a virtuous one. It is one who mingles with in-laws with joy, is courteous to the elders and children alike and serves them, believing them to be equal to gods. You must be obedient and do all the household work yourself. You should know the desires of the elders. Mother-in-law, like a mother, needs your compassion. When we do all of these, gods are pleased with us. I await a time when you shall learn all this and satisfy them all . . . There is a saying amongst us that those poor in industry wreak havoc. Therefore, you should not sit idle but be engaged in work at all times. Serve your mother-in-law and keep your thoughts to yourself. The world is such that people come to us carrying false tales, prise open our mind and, by adding water to the buttermilk, take our story wherever it finds an ear. And, thus, they seize the opportunity wherever there is scope. Therefore, pay no attention to such people and tell them you know nothing. There are nine virtues in not saying anything and twelve faults when we speak. Thus, not knowing a thing is a way to happiness. There is a saying that many come to break a house but no one to build one, therefore, if you want to stay harmoniously at your in-laws', you should follow my path—no matter what is said to us, we must listen to it. And our endeavour should be to foster affection, as we should remain and keep everyone happy. We should not utter a lie and should say nothing to anyone.

In another letter she wrote to you:

Do not share matters of your home with anyone; we should be tight-lipped and keep everything to ourselves. These days, no one can be trusted and you shall be happy if you serve your mother-in-law. The shastras say that there are four parents, which include the parents-in-law. They raised

Himmatbhai and gave him some education, now you have to repay them by being obedient to their commands. They raised him with hardships so that they experience happiness in return in the future. They asked for your hand, hence, it your duty to care for them. You should not fail to do this duty. Do not cultivate friendship with anyone outside the house, you should share the same loving relationship with your mother-in-law that you have with me. I would be satisfied only when your conduct matches with what I have written.

Lilavati! You took these lessons to your heart and gave such satisfaction to the one who gave that advice, but today, she is in deep sorrow and no word of solace or comfort from me can assuage her pain. It is said that things are not desirable or undesirable because of their innate qualities, it is the virtue of the beholder that makes a thing desirable or does not. In some ways, this is correct but, in another way, it suffers from certain non-inclusion. Your virtues would appear desirable to one who is virtuous, while one who lacks virtues would either regard them as undesirable or remain ignorant of them. There was a time when your presence gave us joy and today your absence is the cause of our pain. Is this not excluded from the meaning of that statement? If being with you is desirable and separation from you is undesirable, why did we not feel pain when you were at your in-laws' and why is this separation today so unbearably despicable?

The one who counselled you is in pain and the reason for this is that you followed her advice, but, before you could get the fruit of happiness, you left! You left and yet you proved that the statement of the shastra is true in every sense and in each context. It does not suffer from the fault of non-inclusion. If the fruits of your actions were not your desire while following your mother's advice and if you were not unhappy while following this advice which entailed hardships, then we should deduce that you remained indifferent to the rewards while following the path of duty and virtue. Meanwhile, your mother, who gave you the advice and enjoined upon you the path of duty, is inconsolable and mourns deep in her sorrow today. The one who gave the advice and the one who followed it were persons of different dispositions. Did you really never expect to be rewarded for your actions? Were you never dissatisfied? Your life was one of penance, with spiritual quest. When I look at the core of your being, I see nothing but detachment, harmony and deep satisfaction. You had overcome every sorrow!

On your visit to the hills of Abu, you came to be acquainted with another woman who was unhappy like you and, then, in Palanpur, you met someone else, who was suffering just as you did. During your bouts of 'hysteria', you would call out to them out loud, 'Sister, come here—behn, you too come. All three of us are unhappy, but I will show you a way. Why should we submit to pain? In fact, we should tell pain and unhappiness that they can strike with as much force as they can, but we shall hold on to our happiness. Listen to me, my friends—don't submit to pain at all.'

Lilavati! You knew how to overcome pain and suffering. In this world—a world that is a tempest in the ocean—many are flung hither and tither by waves of pain; but, alas, it seems like neither humans nor gods come to their aid. You too were in a similar situation. In moments like these, when you're utterly helpless, the only source of support is one's own cultivations and faith in God. Those who are unable to see God weep helplessly like an orphan, but those who get to see God are freed from the strings of either happiness or sorrow. The cultivation, faith and this ability to feel the presence of God combine to make self-realisation possible. And you, my child, were able to attain this self-realisation and overcome all pain and suffering. Am I overstating facts? Or does my bias towards you brim my eyes with such thoughts? Or is this, indeed, the truth?

3

You carefully kept my letters of guidance along with your favourite *Savitiri Charitra Natak*.[7] Here is one such letter:

In the process of educating you and teaching you all the household chores, Shastri Maharaj, your

---

[7] *Savitri Charitra Natak*, based on the Sanskrit original by Shighrakavi Shankarlal Moheshwar. Gujarati adaptation by Vishvanath Vitthalji Vaidya and Keshavlal Hariram Bhatt, Bombay, 1881.

mother and I gave you enough grief, but all of that was for your welfare. Similarly, if you face any hardship or feel any pain now, do know that our Father, the Almighty, is putting you through a trial to ensure your future welfare; and just as there is day after every night, He will grant you happiness eventually. It is this faith in God which allows us to retain our composure when facing the hurdles that he places on our way. We must know that if we propitiate God, He will ensure our welfare and help us remain happy and secure in this faith.

We have given you good education and cultivation which can come to your aid when you are separated from us. This knowledge will secure your happiness in another, foreign place. When you are afraid or find yourself in a quandary, just as you used to speak to your mother to seek help, converse with your intellect. This will resolve the knotty problems and show you the right path. Whatever be the situation, you should not be afraid in the least. Having faith in the intent of your family, your knowledge and the presence of God, gain forbearance. If you see someone touched by untruth and impurity, have compassion on that person knowing that such a person has not been granted good knowledge by God. If God had indeed been kind, that person would not have adopted a wrong path. You should be grateful to God that we could give you enough knowledge to not choose the wrong path.

Remind yourself of Gunasundari—what kind of people she was surrounded by and how, using her virtue and tact, she made them her own. Do likewise. Regardless of the other person's character, if we are good and pious, righteousness will ultimately triumph; and, hence, know that eventually God will do good by us.

We have heard praises about you—that you serve your mother-in-law diligently. This fills us with joy, and if you continue to serve her this way, she will bless you and you shall be happy.

If someone speaks harshly to you, don't let it cause unhappiness; your response should be so sweet and delicate that that person will repent—if not today, perhaps tomorrow—and eventually will speak well of you. If you notice anyone's shortcomings, forgive them, do not expose such follies of others to anyone else and caution yourself in a way that you do not acquire such shortcomings. If your mother-in-law finds any fault in you, explain yourself to her with humility and your conduct should be such that she doesn't find further faults in you. This will give both, you and her, happiness.

Your younger *Phua*[8] has sent a copy of *Kadambari* for you which we will get delivered to you.

However, you should not be too perturbed if you don't have the time to read these days. Service to the mother-in-law is a form of education. The benefit that you would have derived from books, I shall compensate through my letters and that would be your education.

---

[8] Paternal aunt's husband; Chhaganlal Harilal Pandya, translator of *Kadambari*.

Here is another letter:

> Moreover, if you don't have the time to read,
> even when you have a moment or two, you
> should try to remember the wise counsel and
> moral lessons from the books that you were
> made to read. Your mother has been shown the
> path of knowledge and you should remember
> how she spends her time in contemplation of the
> divine and happiness that she has secured. You
> should try and secure such joy. Behn, you have
> been separated from us and now you live in a
> foreign place, we cannot go there to either advise
> you or give you knowledge; but make your mind
> stronger with the aid of whatever little education
> we have given to you, so that the suffering of the
> world does not inflict pain and sorrow.

Lilavati! What can I possible say about these
letters? I could not give you any of the benefits that
I had promised. My engagements in Bombay did
not permit me to fulfil my resolve to educate you
through my letters. Your life was imbued with each
word and letter of my advice to such a degree that, as

I sit down to describe your heart and good conduct, all I can say is that each advice your mother and I had given—which were easier said than done—you followed them till the very end of your life with enthusiasm, believing them to be the truth. As I look up towards the sky to ask if there was anything that you did not follow, I see your visage before me. I can say that except for our final desire to see your face at the hour of our death, you fulfilled all the rest of our desires. But that was the fault of all our destinies. And as we mourn the unfulfilled desire, it is the deep attachment we have that is to be blamed. The attachment has been described by a person as learned as King Harishchandra as, 'Oh son! You who slept in my lap was bitten by the cruel fate in form of a serpent even before your life would be fulfilled and that causes me pain.'[9]

A king devoted to truth considered his own bondage to a *chandala* of a lesser significance than his desire to see his son ascend his throne. The death of the son singed him and he called fate cruel.

---

[9] *The Cand-Kaushika of Arya Ksemisvara*, edited and translated by Sibani Das Gupta (Calcutta: The Asiatic Society, 1962), p. 199, Act V, Verse 5.

Lilavati! Is this also why you left us before your life could come to fruition? Should I also accuse cruelty of fate? 'But, O child, you are distressing my heart today; for you, who should have been seated on the lap, have been bitten unexpectedly by the crud serpent of destiny without having fulfilled your duty!' (By cruel fate you have been brought to a grievous fate without fulfilling your duty).[10]

The play *The Cand-Kaushika of Arya Ksemisvara* was among your favourites. If I were to consider you imbued with its lessons, what would your answer be?

4

During your bouts of hysteria, you spoke aloud, conversed with God. 'O, God! Give me as much sorrow as you desire. I do not say no to you. Have I ever shed a tear in disdain to the pain you have given me? I don't blame you for this, because whatever you do, your actions are motivated by good, noble and a larger design. But I do have to ask you about the plague and famine that you send to wreak havoc

---

[10] Ibid.

and kill people in slow and painful death. You must believe these deaths to be necessary but instead of giving people a cruel death why don't you bring an earthquake, a deluge and kill instantly? Is not the second a more preferable way of destruction?'

Lilavati, the humility and the sweetness with which you asked me questions in your conscious state is also the same manner in which you asked God in your coma state. Does not your question show that you considered accusing God or the cruelty of fate improper?

Both Vedanta and Western knowledge believe that thoughts that emanate from the unconscious manifest themselves as dreams. Are not the thoughts of your hysterical state a reflection of the ideas during your state of wakefulness and health? You would accept a path directed by me, even when taking such a path was disagreeable to you. Similarly, God opts for a path disliked by you but your question to him does not sully your faith because, before questioning, you show your willingness to bear with your share of suffering. You reflect compassion and pity for all other beings but, in your own case, you consider it your duty to bear with all the suffering

with peace, equanimity and faith. Everyone—
including me—should do their duties in the manner
in which you did yours. This is the unstated lesson
that you gave us, and remembering this I free myself
of all sorrow and urge your mother and all other
mourning mothers to do likewise. The helplessness
experienced by Harishchandra in the play must not
to be experienced by either me or your mother lest
we, like the king, call fate itself cruel. This is one
of the moral lessons you taught us through your
conduct.

5

Did you not leave before fulfilling your duty? And if
you did, why should I not feel as meek and powerless
as the king in your favourite play? You would
reply, as it was your philosophical disposition, like
Nachiketa, 'I did not desire personal happiness, but
welfare of all'. Women in our society take pleasure
in clothes and jewellery, their life is spent in pursuit
of many domestic desires and men do not allow
them to fulfil their vocation as human beings—they
are incapable of it because they themselves don't

have it in them to do so. When they themselves lack internal resources to fulfil their vocation, how can they enable others to do so? Lilavati, you did not seek to satisfy yourself with material objects in and through which most human beings seek fulfilment. In fact, when you were offered such objects, you refused to have them. You sought the knowledge about as to where your welfare lay and wove it in the fabric of your life. What could be the reason for this?

No human being usually desires death, they seek life. The *shrutis* describe the means to personal comfort as *preya* and humans aspire after such endeavours, in a manner they are capable of for attaining these. Life comes to an end in this endeavour. It is common to find such aspirations and desires in the world.

On the other hand, quite contrary to this, some rare human beings—some great souls—seek fulfilment of human vocation. Their means to fulfil such aspirations differs from the means adopted to secure personal welfare or *preya*. This different undertaking has been described by the *shrutis* as *shreya*. These souls consider human life as a means to attain *shreya*—welfare of all. They do not seek personal happiness; they do not seek pleasure. This makes their life one long penance. The desire to lead a life of penance and their endeavours to secure it is also a form of lust for life. The purpose of a life of penance is fulfilment of duty. So living one fulfils the human vocation. A life not moved by the desire for personal welfare is celebrated by the *shruti* thus: 'Even while doing deeds here, one may desire to live a hundred years.'[11]

And yet one is expected not to be attached to duties either. Lilavati, this is the lesson of the Isa Upanishad, a *shruti* that you loved. You sought fulfilment through the desire for your duty.

6

Just as there is the desire to seek personal happiness and welfare of all, there is also the desire for death. This desire is of two kinds as well—the worldly and the religious duty. This worldly death is called suicide. A person who is moved only by personal

---

[11] Isa Upanishad, verse 2.

pleasure, forced with unbearable sorrow, seeks to alleviate it through ending life itself. Whereas, a person imbued with a sense of religious duty remains distant from this worldly desire with death as a means to escape suffering. This sense of religious duty stems from the performance of duty. The death that a Kshatriya desires on the battlefield is a religious duty to them. While making every effort to be alive, while striving for victory, they do not harbour any fear of death on the battlefield as they enter the jaws of death. The Katha Upanishad says that in obedience to his father's command, Nachiketa awaited Yama—death; he faced death and received wisdom from him. This desire to embrace death is a fitting example of seeking death through performance of duty. This desire for death is born out of a dedication to perform one's duty. The pursuit of duty at times takes one closer to death.

Lilavati, you understood well the desire for life and death as ordained by the *shrutis* and you sought after the fulfilment of duty. This was always a part of your spiritual life, and I have experienced how you did not forsake it till the end of your life. With this knowledge, I consider mourning your loss inappropriate. Your desire for higher life, your sense of religious duty, your penance, your aspirations—all of them I recall. Penance is indifference to pain in performance of duty. The apogee of a life of duty is readiness to embrace death. One lusts for life to the extent that indifference to pain and suffering is not easy to cultivate. Desire for life is also manifest in the quest for happiness while performing one's duties. A life of penance combines both—the quest for happiness and an endeavour to cultivate indifference to pain. When these two contradictory impulses are in balance and one has cultivated detachment to both joy and sorrow, then it is considered a good life—our people have sought to understand life through such and similar other terms and they seek to live through the four stages of life with this knowledge. Poet Akho[12] spoke of this wisdom: 'A wise man plays unfathomable game, his presence remains immortal as the pole star.'

---

[12] Akha Bhagat, or Akha Rahiyadas Soni (c. 1615–c. 1674), commonly known as Akho, was a medieval Gujarati poet who wrote in the tradition of Bhakti in a literary form called *Chhappa* (six stanza poems). *Akhe-gita* is considered as an important work.

This author has witnessed the endeavours of a delicate young woman, who, though tender in age, had attained heights of perseverance. Lilavati, you played this unfathomable play as naturally as fish plays in water and then disappeared—which I also witnessed. For many reasons, it is impossible to present an unsullied picture of that dream. As I think of that dream, I cannot but repent. And yet readers have praised and welcomed a work of fiction by this author and they will find what he has experienced both dear and instinctive. So, believing that, I have embarked upon this work.

2

The Confluence of the Sources of Life

7

Lilavati was betrothed at the age of three or four to Rajman Himmatbhai, the third son of Rajman Rajashir Manibhai Gangashankar Shakkawala, who hailed from the town of Petlad situated in the territories of the Gaikwad State. The family, once very wealthy, had come under pecuniary strain during Ra. Ra. Manibhai's middle age. According to the norms set by Lilavati's caste, marriages had to be fixed in the same town in which her parents resided. The thought of marrying their daughters off to a distant, foreign place and the separation that it entailed from their beloved daughters made the hearts of the loving parents tremble with pain. As per the customs here, any delay in the betrothing turned out to be detrimental to the girls, because a girl's happiness has to be sought by selecting a husband elder to her. A husband has to be selected from amongst boys born before the girl and the number of such boys will reduce with the birth of a girl child who are betrothed at the earliest opportunity. Hence, as seen in many castes, including the one to which this author belongs, such delay in betrothal harms the interests of the girl. Given the paucity of suitable grooms for Lilavati in Nadiad, the idea of getting her betrothed to a family residing elsewhere seemed like a possibility, and soon this idea was implemented. This break from an age-old custom did cause some rift among those whose self-interests were compromised. But that cannot be helped. Eventually, they too joined the others in this practice and since then many girls from Vadnagara Nagar Brahmin families have been married into families in Petlad, Surat and Kathiawad, while girls from Surat have been married into Nadiad families.

At one point in time, Ra. Manibhai was quite a wealthy man and his riches and generosities were widely praised. But some thirty-five to forty years ago, after the stock market crashed, his firm collapsed, and with the burden of debt coupled with financial crisis, he started some share brokerage and another business in Bombay. He had secured the affection of Sheth Premachand Roychand,[1] but his destiny did not change for the better. The revered father of this author had also experienced indebtedness and impoverishment of which the author had personal experience. In fact, the author himself was betrothed at a time when he was faced with such hardships. So, when the close relatives objected to Lilavati's betrothal in a family that faced

---

[1] Premchand Roychand (1831–1906), pioneering businessman, known as 'cotton king' and 'bullion king' of Bombay, founding member of The Native Share and Stock Broker Association, known as the Bombay Stock Exchange, made significant capital gains during the cotton boom triggered by the American Civil War, endowed the Rajbai Clock Tower in the University of Bombay and the Premchand Roychand Scholarship (PRS) in the University of Calcutta.

such a pecuniary crisis, this author thought of his own condition. Despite our financial crisis, my father-in-law had placed his trust in my family and if I have similar trust in Manibahi's family, I don't have the right to consider their improvised state. The confidence came from the conviction that a bright student would make a better husband than a man with wealth.

At the time of my wedding during our financial crisis and impoverished condition, my dear sister had composed a ditty: 'I have seen all the students there are to be seen, no other is a match to my brother, come check him out.'

I know that I was nothing but a mediocre student, but the confidence that my youngest sister Samarth Laxmi had in my capabilities had me filled with enthusiasm. Among the eligible boys from our caste, Himmatbhai was the best student. Having determined this, Lilavati was betrothed to him. Sister Samarth Laxmi was in many ways partial towards Lilavati and the niece was promised in marriage as desired by her aunt. Given all these factors, the impoverished condition of her father-in-law was not considered an obstacle. My impoverished condition did not make my sister meek or dejected. She praised her brother for his learnings. My heart sought to imitate her. But that sister of mine is no more, my daughter too is gone. But as fate willed, that family has remained in an impoverished state. Some thirty-five years after his firm collapsed, at the age of seventy-five, Ra. Manibhai does a small job due to the kindness of the state officials in Junagadh. He is still not free of debt. Pecuniary hardships shortened the studentship of Himmatbhai who has begun legal practice in Junagadh. His fate was ahead of him and there were years of famine in Junagadh. Before his legal practice—which started well with help of relatives—could flourish, and he could free his father from the burden of debt, years of famine commenced. The debt remained. Before the effects of famine on legal practice could be erased, Lilavati became a patient to tuberculosis.

The poverty which became integral to Lilavati's life was a gift of her father's logic! This story intends to show how she dealt with her impoverished condition with equanimity.

8

One evening, after we were satiated by a meal cooked by Lilavati, she began a conversation. She asked softly, 'Mota Kaka, how did the vegetable and the dal taste today?'

'Good.'

'That's great!' (She laughed a little.)

Her mother then spoke up, 'Lilavati cheated us today. She did not add turmeric to the two items she had made.'

Lilavati then went on to explain, 'Mota Kaka, lack of turmeric did not alter the taste. The colour that it adds was not missed at night. Is it wrong to save the expense and not use it for the evening meal?'

'So, this is how you experiment at your in-laws?' I asked.

'Could be,' answered Lilavati.

'Behn, that's all right. But turmeric has a property that cleanses our blood.' She was somewhat disappointed to learn about the properties of turmeric. Her mother added, 'She tries all such clever tricks at her in-laws', and I did warn her. She thought that she would be able to have her way with you but your response has defeated her.'

Lilavati! You were not defeated, you won. You were dejected but that dejection for me was a sign of hope. But the hope came to a naught in this transient world. The poet had depicted such hope for the eternal world in *Amar Asha*[2] and my hope became one with that eternal hope.

9

What was the reason for this feeling of dejection? Was it her meekness which stopped her to become free of challenges? On another occasion, she had asked her mother, 'When I step out of the house, I make sure I wear clothes that do not harm the prestige of our family, but is it wrong to use less of ghee and milk considering the condition of my in-laws?' The minute calculations of expenses and careful dressing up to preserve the honour

[2] A well-known Gujarati ghazal of by the philosopher Manilal Nabhubhai Diwvedi (1858–1898), a contemporary of Govardhanram, also a resident of Nadiad.

were not things that Lilavati had learnt at our home, she learnt that at her in-laws'. One of the wedding vows include: 'I will look at what is and is not at the in-laws' house'. This vow of *Saptapadi* was not explained to Lilavati but her heart sought it out and she shaped her conduct accordingly. Would someone like her not feel dejected if she were to not succeed in her attempts? Lilavati was determined to live parsimoniously at her in-laws' and she declined every help that I offered. Lilavati was determined not to be eclipsed by the poverty of her in-laws. She resolved to fight it. She believed that whatever little wealth that our family possessed was rightfully her brother's and she did not allow any one to circumscribe the right of her brother in any way. She would caution her mother, 'Ba! Be careful! Don't believe that you daughter is like other daughters in our society. You would commit a crime before God if you were to favour me more than my brother and sister-in-law. Teach your daughters to be content with their own destinies.' Lilavati's lust for life found manifestation in three things: a sense of contentment in her impoverished state, joy at that contentment and hope for a better future. And, as a part of that lust for life, as a response to her condition, as a means to attaining a better tomorrow, she led a parsimonious life; did not spend too much on 'ghee and milk' and she experimented all such tricks on herself. This disposition, this endeavour, may be called penance or by another name. But the experiment failed as she realised that life also needed blood-purifying turmeric. She was required to seek out a new experiment. She accepted both the dejection, owing to the failed experiment, and the worry to find a new experiment in parsimony. Her dejection was a sign for me that she desired life and her concern would force her to look for new ways. That was my hope. Till her death, Lilavati tried to fulfil this hope in a variety of ways. Eclipsed by her fate she did not cease action This incessant striving is characteristic of our people which embodies the cherished *amar asha*—eternal hope. The belief that our endeavours will make death gift us its fruits in another life is an eternal hope. Ordinary people sometimes surrender themselves to their fate; eclipsed by the vicissitudes of life, they desire death, seek profit through sinful means and are rendered incapacitated like the cow that finds herself incapable of either fighting or fleeing when forced to face the lion's roar; they lead a life of misery and timidity. *Tamas*, darkness, arises and desire for life is sullied by such darkness. Lilavati's injunction to her mother demonstrated her resolve to remain unsullied by such darkness. This distance, this resolution to remain unsullied, harboured her hope for welfare. That desire for welfare could either be for *preya*—personal pleasure—or for the ennobling *shreya*. Such is an endeavour which seers sow as hope and faith.

10

How was Lilavati to be rescued from her situation? She declined to accept anything more that what is customarily given to daughters as per our family's tradition and caste. If any attempt was made to give her more than the customary gifts, she would ascertain if her sisters too were given those additional gifts, and she denied everything that her sisters were not given. She considered this violation of norms and firmly refused to be party to such violations. One of her notebooks—where the first page had her handwritten inscription 'My dear book' in English—contains a page on which in large letters the following is written: 'It is a duty to follow the commands of elders but God is supreme among elders and one is not to follow any injunctions of parents or any other elders if it is in violation of the command of God'. This was her sense of duty and morality which she ardently followed. On the one hand, we saw her attempts to spend less on ghee and milk and suffer privations and, on the other, she denied to accept anything additional that her mother and I tried to give her, as this to her was violation of norms. How were we to establish this as righteous? What were we to do with a daughter who believed that her duty was to remain tied to the fate of her in-laws? After much thought, this author remembered how Lilavati had the latent ability to write books, this, he decided, should be nurtured to generate additional income for a secure future. In fact, this would have given her both money and fame, her soul would have found joy and, moreover, nothing could prevent me from buying out copies that remained unsold! I decided that the last part of the plan should be kept from her but the rest should be discussed with her when she came to Nadiad from Junagadh. But who was I, a father proud of his daughter, to decide this plan? God willed otherwise. When she came to Nadiad, her physical condition had deteriorated out of our hands. She was examined by the doctor the very next day and he detected tuberculosis creeping through her body. The doctor's diagnosis broke her mother's heart and she wept a flood of tears. The news made Lilavati's heart hard like the indestructible *vajra*. Experiencing the fear of death or the physical pain from the disease did not make her lose courage or plead, it did not make her mind eclipse or express helplessness. From that day till her death, a year later, except at times of extreme physical pain, she did not shed tears in her conscious state. It was her resolve to not weep.

11

'Lilavati, does anyone at your in-laws' know about your experiments with turmeric?' I had asked.

'No, Mota Kaka. Before implementing it there, I began the experiment at our home.'

'Behn! All your experiments and observations began from my home!'

'Ba! If I were to drink milk here, I would need milk there as well. I will make attempts to come out of that habit here itself, hence don't force me.'

'Ba, no one says a no to anything that I wish to eat at my in-laws'. They have given all the responsibilities to me. But such habits must begin at the natal home itself, so that one is appreciated later at her in-laws'.'

For those daughters who aspire to pleasures, there is a saying—a feast in the grandfather's house and one's mother to serve the food makes one satiated. You considered this wisdom to be contrary to the right conduct. But, Lilavati, only you, who had overcome desire for pleasure, found it your duty to prevent your mother from giving anything excess to you in your own home. There is a saying of the shastras about conduct at the in-laws' house: 'A wife who squanders is an enemy of the husband.' You had understood and taken to heart the duty of wife of an impoverished man and you wanted your parents to know that you were aware of your duties and that this was not a cause of deep dissatisfaction for you. Did you not play little tricks with us so that we too were not unhappy with your condition and resolve? O, you devoted truth! If I had asked you this question while you were alive, I am certain that you would have said nothing in response and brushed the question aside.

12

What about your internal resources, what of your education and cultivation that allowed you to accept the poverty of your in-laws? And how did you decide to engage with what others consider undesirable and hence subject to disdain? If I were to consider poverty your enemy, I see that you had forgiven that enemy. I can see the greatness and generosity of your heart when I see the others whom you had similarly forgiven. Just some days—or maybe a few months—before your death, I saw you sitting alone with your mother. And, that Lilavati, who did not shed a tear even when crushed by the burden of sorrows, that Lilavati, who had resolved not to weep, was shedding copious tears!

'Lilavati! What is this?' I had asked. Your mother, in response, expressed her regret. She explained what had caused her heart to boil over. 'That thing angered me and I said something disdainful about her mother-in-law. And Moti has been weeping ever since.'

'Lilavati! Is that true?' I asked, after which she wept even more and replied, 'Mota Kaka, yes, it is true. But what about that? My mother-in-law is not learned, she is weak and meek. She knows that her happiness is related to mine, but she does not have the ability to clearly comprehend this. But who was the one to utter such harsh words? My mother—one who has been educated by you, the one who taught me my duties towards my mother-in-law. That very mother said such words! How am I to bear this?'

I had no answer to give and I turned away. Lilavati! What could I have said in response? How was I to blame your mother's love for you, which taught you your duties but despised the outcome of the performance of duty? I am rendered speechless by this. Should it surprise one that you were angry when your mother-in-law was criticised, which for you was itself a violation of duty? I could find no fault with you. You would forgive your mother and she would not cause you to weep again—of that too

I was certain. I left the two of you to your affection and duty and turned away. Your wisdom would in your last moments give you other-worldly courage, this thought was a source of solace for me, and my heart melted and continues to do so as I witnessed your affection, generosity for your mother-in-law. Your wealth consisted of such intangible and subtle emotions. A month or so after your death, your mother-in-law too died. If you were alive at the time of her death, how pained would you have been! Many daughters-in-law take delight at the death of the mother-in-law, how dismissive would you have been of them! The wisdom of Sita did not allow her to see anything unpleasant about Rama's banishment to the forest; similarly wise one, the poverty of your husband and his family did not in any way reduce your affection for them and allowed you to garner in the face of poverty the wealth of subtle emotions.

13

How did Lilavati, enriched by her intangible wealth, serve her mother-in-law? Once, when she visited us for an occasion after her marriage, her mother accused her of disobedience to her mother-in-law. This author was required to adjudicate the matter. In her defense, Lilavati had said, 'Mota Kaka, in all matters, save one, I obey my mother-in-law. Many a time, she desires something but her words are contrary to her desires. In such instances, rather than obeying her words, I do what I know to be her heart's desires. Apart from this, I do obey her in all the matters.'

Lilavati, you understood the *Manojnadharma*, the duty to follow the unsaid wishes of others. Such was your affection. Lilavati! Under what notion of justice was I to ask you to give up such subtle richness of your mind? Our women know the duty of understanding the wishes of others and act in accordance with them. I had imagined such observances among the ascetics of Sundargiri,[3] which you personified. When my wretched heart thinks of this, I forget your pain and sorrow and see this light installed in

---

[3] A community of ascetics, both male and female, imagined by Govardhanram in the fourth part of *Sarasvatichandra*.

the temple of heart which dispels the darkness produced by sorrow. This light gives me solace. Your mother often accused you of such violation but your defence in each instance triumphed over the accusations. Your light uplifted your mother, gave me immense satisfaction both through your words and conduct.

'Lilavati, where is your saree?' One day, your mother asked.

Lilavati smiled and said, 'Ba, you had gifted me that saree, isn't it?'

'Yes, but where have you kept it?'

'Ba, I was told that in our caste there is no custom of giving gifts to the mother-in-law. That must be your custom, but am I to seek your consent if I wish to give her something that is mine? She did not ask for it. But I am happy that she has it. I can do without it.'

Lilavati understood the unsaid desire of her mother-in-law and gave her the saree, she did not; disclose the person who had gifted it to her but ensured that the gift was accepted. She rose above the desire for possession and acted as a medium to satisfy her mother-in-law's desires.

14

When her mother criticised her mother-in-law, she wept like a child and, on another instance, on hearing criticism of her husband, she roared like a lioness from her sick bed. Her grandmother and some other women had clustered around her bed and one of them spoke ill of her husband in the context of her disease. As the words reached her ears, she chided her grandmother, 'Motiba, if someone speaks ill of one's husband, that person should be beheaded isn't it?' These words from a very ill person stunned everyone, just as the roar of a lion silences other animals. The heartfelt roar of a virtuous woman silenced the elderly women. She did not wait to consider social norms, nor did the presence of her elderly grandmother deter her. She did not pause to consider her response, her heart defended what she worshipped, and those words captured the essence of her feelings.

15

Her devotion to her husband also forced her to forsake her resolve to not seek her father's help and place a burden on him. A prolonged famine and draught in Junagadh and excessive rains one monsoon resulted in the epidemic of the fever. A friend has described the epidemic: 'From the servant of God, the Nawab Sahib, to the humblest resident of the state, there is not one family which does not have at least one—child or elder—suffering from the fever. Some even die from it.'

Lilavati's in-laws, one after the another, were gripped by the fever. Doctor Chhaganlal Gulabdas Kazi had great affection for the family, but there was no relief from the fever even after his ministrations. Finally, a weary Lilavati wrote to her mother, 'Ba, I know that Pitaji is now retired and it is not the time to place additional burdens on him. But now there is no option but a change in air, that would be the only cure. The only way is for the two of us to come to Nadiad. If you were to write to me, inviting us there, I can tell him about it and then the two of us can come. We have burdened you in times when you had the means, and now, for another six months, we shall burden you again. You could consider this as a part of the charity that you do.' Lilavati's mother came to me with the letter. What other response could there be to such a letter?

When Vishwamitra asked Harishchandra for a gift, Harishchandra replied, 'Even the whole world is not gift enough for thee. With my ability not sufficing (even) by a gift of all possessions, I offer to thee now. O son of Kaushika, this entire earth with all its wealth.'[4] And Lilavati, given her sense of duty and her own resolve, had hitherto taken not even that was due to her. When she gave up her resolve and sought something so little, what response could there be, except one? She was not worried about herself but about the fate of her husband and hence sought our help. 'Himmatbhai should be invited here without further delay, write a letter to him and another to Lilavati,' I said.

Lilavati, this was the only thing that you ever asked of me in your short life, and this request was an act of grace and kindness. The subtle richness of your heart gave me this boon of your kindness

---

[4] *The Cand Kaushika of Arya Ksemisvara*, edited and translated by Sibani DasGupta (Calcutta: The Asiatic Society, 1962), p. 169, Act II.

and at this juncture of living in separation from you, this became a source of solace for me. 'Lilavati, you and the one who rules your heart, come, come immediately to our home!' My good fate permitted me to write this but our ill-fortune also lurked behind. Lilavati could not come immediately. After a great effort, she came with her husband and mother-in-law. When she finally did, the condition of her body broke our heart and the very next day the doctor diagnosed that the germs of tuberculosis had entered her heart.

16

The moment her mother heard the diagnosis, her heart which was filled with love for her daughter came to be filled with bad omens and trembled at the calamity that lay ahead. Her eyes welled up with tears. 'The disease is at the preliminary stage and can be cured,' the doctor gave hope. Her mother too had once contracted tuberculosis and had been cured. This gave hope to her heart. She dried her tears and sought duty in remedies prescribed by the doctor. But Lilavati was not in the least perturbed by the diagnosis, instead, she became composed. She had read about tuberculosis and, therefore, she thought about her condition calmly. She gave up worrying about her in-laws and became deeply careworn about her parents. It was futile to consider a return to the in-laws till she was entirely cured of the tuberculosis. And she stopped worrying about what was futile. So long as her skeleton-like body could serve her in-laws, she remained duty-bound, but as she became incapable of performing the duty, she became free from that concern. Now she had to take medication day and night and submit to the regime of the doctor. For one year, she lived in a condition where her body was incapacitated and at mercy of others, but she did not complain, she did not hesitate in taking all that was prescribed to her and eschew all that was proscribed. She took many medications that were distasteful on the tongue, knowing at all times that all the efforts might eventually fail. She gave solace and patience to all those who had loved her. Himmatbhai, who was with her, and the others at her in-laws' place, she did not let her foreboding touch them. To her parents who were aware of the dangers that lay ahead, she tried to give comfort and solace. Her concern for the health of her husband had forced her to give up on her resolve of not seeking her father's help. Her delicate heart also opened up to her mother and shared the nature of duties she had performed at her in-laws', something that she had hitherto avoided.

'Ba, in those days of fever epidemic, there were only two possible outcomes. If I had cared for myself and not him, he would have certainly lost his life. I did not put myself first and now what has to become of me, will! Ba, either he would have lost his life or I would have, this was certain. What has happened is for the better. Ba, don't worry, don't mourn, you take such care of me, Mota Kaka does so much, spends so much on my medication. It will do good. But, if that is not what the God has willed, know that either he would have gone or I, and it is I who is to go. You would have seen me inhabiting a corner of the house as a widow, but you will see me go as a married woman, which is a sign of your good fortune. Ba, remember this and do not mourn. Is there anything that could possibly be done to cure me that you have not tried?' Lilavati could not bring herself to say this to her mother all at once, she could not ever keep this from her mother, and she shared this over many conversations when the time was opportune. What is written above is a summation of what she had said. She sought health for her husband even at the cost of endangering her life. O Lilavati, you did this deliberately, and were not scared of the danger, the inevitable outcome. You did not wallow in sorrow or repent your action. You accepted the danger and that was the fulfilment of your duty. Lilavati! The path of duty that your parents had showed brought you like Nachiketa to the door of death and in death you sought fulfilment. You gave your mother the right to glimpse into your ennobling life and through her I too had the opportunity and good fortune to do likewise.

Oh virtuous one! You sought health for your husband and death for yourself! This was the zenith of your duties towards the in-laws! The pinnacle of your subtle riches.

There is a saying that a trumpet heralds the uncountable wealth. This was the trumpet that announced your unseen, non-tangible wealth.

I comfort myself by hearing that trumpet and watching the summit. I think back and know that while you were healthy you did not accept anything from your parents, but once you fell ill we did all we could for your treatment. You accepted the care, even asked for it. I recognise that you did not do this because you loved your life but knew that your fate had carried you to the house of death and you wanted to give your parents the solace and satisfaction of giving you every possible treatment and care so that they did not have to live with the thorns in their hearts. I realised that during the period of your illness.

17

All humans acquire a sense of religious duty that binds them. Performance of duty is according to their capacity, condition and capabilities that they have acquired. For some, physical instincts dominate over religious duty and, for others, physical instincts remain subjugated to the religious duty. Those who are not bound by religious duty remain subject to physical passions, those who give up physical passions attain bonds of duty. Both bind but bondage to physical passions give joy as well as sorrow while religious duty gives a sense of harmony and balance. Both joy and sorrow eclipse before religious bonds. Those subject to bodily passions become meek of heart and distance themselves from the divine, while those hearts which are imbued with religious duty remain free of meekness and acquire the presence of the divine that makes them fit to receive grace and work for the welfare of others.

Lilavati, imbued with a sense of religious duty, did not become poor because of her impoverished state; agony could not eclipse her and, surrounded by the darkness of poverty, she lit the golden lamp of subtle wealth. Not only women but also men crushed by the burdens of hardships and misfortunes turn melancholic and weep or take the path of sin. Lilavati who was under similar burden remained intent upon the divine which fulfilled her life through good actions and gave her soul that strength. This light filled her with so much richness that whether she was around her parents or her in-laws, she exuded her inner richness.

Lilavati! When you left home, a certain sum was given to you, that remains outstanding against your name. Please inform Icchashankar how much of that has been spent and what remains as a balance. The amount spent will be accounted for accordingly.

Lilavati, the day of your return is approaching. Please inform Icchashankar of the balance on hand and ask him for the money that you want.

Whenever Lilavati visited, conversation of this kind would take place and she always had much difficulty in responding to such questions. Instead of two columns of expenditure and balance on hand, she had three. 'Balance on hand, money that should be accounted as balance but not in my possession and expenses.' Such was her way of accounting. Whenever she left, she would ask, 'Unless the money that should be shown as outstanding against me has been so entered, I do not want to take anything. If it shows as debit against me, I would ask if I need more.' She was firm that the money she took should be shown as debit against her name, if it was not, she would not take an additional paisa. She would not budge from her resolve and not take money even for petty expenses and seek permission to return to her in-laws. After a long time, she explained the reason for her insistence, to her mother, who failed to understand it and hence she was asked to explain again.

'Mota Kaka, I do spend some money in that house and sometimes I use not their family's money but the money given by you.'

'Does your mother-in-law or someone else know of this?'

'No, no one—they think I spend their money.'

'If you don't let them know how would they appreciate you or thank you for what you do?'

'Mota Kaka, let it be. Who needs appreciation or thanks? It would do good to those for whom it has been spent. I know their situation.'

'Will you repay what you ask us to debit from your account?'

'A part of that I have given to someone, which will be returned once he overcomes his difficulties. For the rest, we shall see.'

Lilavati kept the scales of judgement regarding what should be accounted as expenses of her father and the amount of debt that she had incurred. She had hoped to pay off her debts to me from what was her *stree-dhan*, which was rightfully hers. She considered it her right and duty to gift from that without seeking anyone's permission. This was the generosity and goodness that her sense of duty had bestowed upon her and, though poor herself, she had the capacity to be charitable to others. Given her sense of commitment for the welfare of others, she could do good to all those who'd come within the ambit of her religious duty. Harming others is a demonic desire and even a child is capable of setting fire to a palace, whereas, both the desire and the capability of doing good for others is not acquired easily; the acquisition of both is not possible without the grace of God. The *shrutis* speak of the similarities between the divine and the human and the goodness of divinity obtained by a human only when the two unite. She did not seek fame, did not seek acknowledgement from those who were benefited by her virtue. She remained poor but from her negligible resources (for someone poor, her negligible wealth is priceless, because that's all she has), she desired to make a gift and yet remain unknown. When I saw the light of the subtle soul that resided in her physical body, my head bowed in reverence. To whom did I bow? To that light which emanated from Lilavati's heart.

18

How did Lilavati wish to pay back the amount that she wanted to be shown as outstanding against her? She considered it violation of her sense of rectitude to seek anything from mother and father, and the condition of her in-laws was such that she could not have asked for anything from them. Her eyes were on her *stree-dhan*—pallu[5]—which according to custom was deposited in my custody. Around the time that I decided to leave my practice in Bombay, Lilavati wrote me a letter in which she made an unspecific demand: 'Pitaji, once you had told me that when I become an adult, you will allow me to take one decision. Would you allow me to do as I wish?' I replied, 'Behn, I can respond to this only when I know what is it that you desire.' She wrote back with

---

[5] Pallu is colloquial Gujarati for *stree-dhan*.

a clear statement of her intent: 'You know about the condition of my father-in-law. He has incurred debts and creditors come seeking their due and speak in an unmeasured tone, which is unbearable to me. Therefore, give me my pallu, which I can use to help him. This would give solace to my heart.' She had also hoped to repay what she considered her debt to me through the same pallu. When she expressed her desire to free her in-laws from their debt, the condition of her heart, her emotional life was rather delicate. I could not have fulfilled her desire without violating my duty to Lilavati and her share of wealth. If I had said no, there was a danger that I would break her heart. We decided to defer the matter till we met and discussed, which I hoped would give me and her an opportunity to clarify the matter. After I left Bombay and reached Nadiad, at the first available opportunity she broached the matter.

'Mota Kaka, do you have an objection to this?'

What was I to do when she meekly asked for her share of wealth, which was her religious right?

'Lilavati, I might agree to what you suggest but the very purpose of making parents the custodian of *stree-dhan* is that the in-laws do not claim it and it remains for the use of the daughter.'

'But this is what I want, no one has asked for this.'

'If I were to give you what you ask, this would become an example and other daughters would be coerced by their in-laws, thus, starting an undesirable custom. Lilavati, in caste and community behaviour, it doesn't take long for such practices to take root. The curse of all such daughters would be upon me and you. What do you say to that?'

She was deep in thought.

'We got you married outside Nadiad, how many other girls were so married eventually, citing your example? Customs are formed in this way. I know that you are not worried about yourself, but should this matter not deserve your consideration?'

She stood holding on to a window frame and said nothing. After some time, she went away without giving any response. Lilavati! You understood subtle duties and were compassionate. After a lot of deliberation, I destroyed your resolve to give away all your *stree-dhan* by an argument that pointed at other dangers of your proposed actions. You were dejected as the edifice you had built crumbled from its foundation. You were disappointed but from that disappointment you sought new hope. You found a way, whereby, some money of the in-laws could be saved and you would also not be cursed by other daughters. You decided without informing anyone at the in-laws to spend some of your money and eventually hoped to pay me back from your pallu. If I had said, 'I will put it as expense and not as dues to be recovered from you', you would have stopped withdrawing the money and the doors of hope that your heart had opened would have been shut. I decided to accept your suggestion for the time being and intended to account them as expenses once your fate turned and a new sun shone on your destiny. Eventually, both of us faced dejection. Because you went away before your hope could be actualised. I could not fulfil my plan of helping you either; you withdrew only a part of your *stree-dhan*. This disappointment makes me melancholic. If I had done as Lilavati desired, would that have given her satisfaction? Would that have opened her fate to new possibilities? If her fate had changed, would it not have given her an extended life? She was like Gunasundari of my imagination and, like her, she had the desire to do good for the family. Were my reasons in not assisting her appropriate? Why did I not think of fulfilling her desire from my own meager savings? Did I not think of this because of the miserliness of my heart? All these thoughts and arguments were futile. My melancholy lifts somewhat at the fruitlessness of this contemplation. If my Lilavati were alive, she would have resolved this quandary and, in some ways, she did that as well. Some days before her death she looked at her infant son and told him and her mother, 'Ba, you know what I wanted to do with my pallu. But now, all of it belongs to him.'

Of course! Lilavati! Of course! At a time when your son was not born, you had expressed the desire to spend your pallu on your in-laws. But, considering the possibility of a future when you would have a child of your own, I prevented you from spending all your money as you desired. I do not feel unduly perturbed now that you yourself expressed your desire to use this wealth to secure the future of your infant son. You wanted to free your in-laws from debt. They also have some duties towards this son of yours who is a ray of hope for them. I did manage to provide some aid in this endeavour, which is the twin of what you had initially desired. A mother has a duty towards her child, she has a debt to pay there as well, and the path you chose to secure this future was towards fulfilling that duty. This duty is in some ways larger than the duty of compassion that you had chosen for yourself. I did my duty by allowing you the means to fulfil this greater duty. The words you said to your mother at the hour of your death, I believe, justifies my actions. Your heart was filled with compassion towards your in-laws, while I made my heart hard, both were forms of duty. Both are different forms of the same light. But the form that arose from your heart appears to me more beautiful and divine.

19

After Lilavati's death, in a letter to this author from a family friend who was well versed with the fourth part of *Sarasvatichandra*, two lines of which capture the essence of that divine life:

It is really 'passing strange and wonderful'[6] that the budding blossoms of both the sexes of our present society, writhing under the *Samprayatmak* (based on conviction) system of conventional life, thus, wither and fade like martyrs of *Purusha Yajna* (Supreme Sacrifice) before their prime.[7]

The ancient sages, guided by a variety of reasons, have given us as heritage the *Kama Shastra* for householders. In that, a form of love that is based on affection and conviction is called *Samprayatmak*. It is not the place to debate whether the choices made by the parents for the welfare of their daughters are truly so or not. This question was posed by a little Lilavati at a time when she lacked the capability of comprehending the response. But following the eternal duties of the ascetics, she fulfilled her duties of sacrifice and, on the altar of that sacrificial fire, she offered herself as an oblation. Her father who witnessed her sacrifice and knows the core of her

---

[6] 'Queen Mab', Percy Bysshe Shelly.
[7] Letter from J. M. Buch, 21 January 1902, original in English.

spiritual life can say that like the primal sacrifice she was both the host and the oblation offered in the sacrifice. Like a child who when asleep and awake keeps her doll by her side, Lilavati kept the *Savitri Natak* as her constant companion. Dear readers, this father has been a witness to this and hence you would not consider his statement of faith in her as a statement of partiality.

20

Lilavati, who would other herself as a sacrifice, was not only moved by a sense of obligation and duty but also by a deep sense of love. This can be better explained with description of some incidents. Women have a natural, instinctive fascination for clothes and ornaments. This inclination is a part of their emotional life. Lilavati's mother assumed that Lilavati also had this fascination and would worry about clothes and ornaments for her. Lilavati's mother often kept in check or at times even forwent her own desires to collect new and fancier clothes befitting our family custom for Lilavati and would give them to her when she returned to her in-laws. But when she visited our home again, the clothes would be found unused. Her mother, naturally curious, asked, 'What is the reason?' Lilavati replied meekly, 'Ba, this is the wealth of your home. I would wear such clothes only when the condition of my in-laws improves. Ba! The clothes of that family are more appropriate from me.' Until the time the fate of her in-laws turned, Lilavati, moved by conviction that the time was not right, kept the clothes given to her by her mother aside for a better time. She felt dejected at the disappointment of her mother. She made sure that she did not wear such clothes and in so doing so, she showed the wealth of her affection. She, without any effort, kept in check her desire for gratification. She was proud of what she had and the condition that she was in. Other women would feel the brunt of poverty when denied clothes and ornaments, but Lilavati was dejected that her denial caused pain to her mother.

'Lilavati, you should familiarise yourself with all these boxes,' her mother would tell her. Lilavati in response would say, 'Ba, let Jasubehn be familiar with them, give me something else to do.'

73

What was the reason for Lilavati's indifference to the wealth of her father's home until the time her in-laws' condition improved? Her heart was so invested in the feelings for her in-laws that, moved by love, she made that her home. Some women accept the riches of either the parents or the in-laws and revel in them and are not attracted to the relatively poorer members of the families. But Lilavati not only remained indifferent to the materialistic pleasures of her father's family, but she also took pride in the poverty of her in-laws to an extent that she did not want the fancier materials of her father's home to colour her perspective and kept them at a distance. She was eager and intent upon her indifference to material objects and she remained unmoved by the sacrifice that it entailed.

3

Yajamandharma in Father's House

21

Such were the emotions that governed Lilavati's life at her in-laws. You lived a life of noble sacrifice in your marital home. In fact, her life at her parent's house, too, was driven by similar emotions. She did not ever say, 'This is my right and I shall have it.' For most people, parental home is a place from where they get things, but for her, it was a place to give. When she had no material objects to give, she gave intangible riches. She knew that her parents were worried on her account. She ensured that our worries were lessened. She also cared for us in ways that showed her eagerness and industry.

<h2>22</h2>

Her care and concern were evident in all instances—large and small. After she was diagnosed with tuberculosis, her futile anxieties about the condition of her in-laws had to be laid to rest. But then began her new and unending apprehension about her parents. She knew her parents' heart, she gave them hope that she would eventually get well and till her death she made attempts to secure our emotions. At the same time, she assumed that her death was inevitable and she made attempts to take care of our emotional state in the course of her ailment. She would tell us that her body would endure and even point out signs of improvement. While, at the same time, she would explain to us the appropriate nature of the response expected from us, if God willed otherwise.

'Ba, just because I talk and walk about, do not think that this body will endure this ailment. I have read about tuberculosis; one may die mid-sentence.' One day, she said this in jest and then turned grave and continued, 'Ba, you and Mota Kaka do so much for me and I will be well again. But, if you were to lose courage now, can your body deal with graver concerns later? That's why I said that.'

Every eight or ten days, sometimes even after four-five days, she would look at her mother and advise, sometimes she would even scold her. Her advice was always the same: 'Ba, *Foi's* daughter, Rasika, died of tuberculosis. She mourns her death because she is illiterate. Mota Kaka arranged for *shastris* to teach you and you are knowledgeable. Is it proper for you to worry? Look at Mota Kaka—what forbearance!' Her mother would again turn meek and dark and Lilavati would counsel her again. She never missed an opportunity to guide her.

This author's childhood friend, now deceased, Ra. Maganlal Laxmilal Desai, once came to Nadiad. His younger son died and in the same year his elder son Jayantilal BA died of cholera. Jayantilal had lived in our house for some years as a brother to Lilavati and studied in Bombay. In Ahmedabad, he edited and published as monthly magazine *Arunodaya*. He never missed an opportunity to forcefully advocate my case in face of any criticism.

I had hopes from Jayantilal—whom we used to call Babu at home—given his affection, ability and aspiration for a literary life. Lilavati was aware of our hopes. One need not say how shattered Maganlal was at the death of such an able son.

Maganlal asked Lilavati about her health and they chatted for a while. As he moved away from her side, Lilavati said to her mother, 'Ba! What equanimity and patience Maganlal Kaka has as he deals with Babu bhai's loss! Your pain is negligible compared to his.' In her personal notebook, Lilavati had noted: 'When faced with pain, we should look at someone whose pain is deeper.'

Lilavati had pointed out to her mother both the pain and equanimity of Maganbhai. When the late Dewan of Bhavnagar, Samaldas Parmanandas, met me after Lilavati's death, he recalled his own days of suffering and grief and sought to assuage the grief of this author.

23

We have already noted her attitude towards clothes and ornaments given her affection and sense of duty towards her in-laws. During her healthy years, Lilavati had been indifferent to clothes and ornaments. Her attitude changed after she was diagnosed with the disease. Her words and actions pointed to one thing: 'So far I have steadfastly refused to wear new clothes and ornaments and, after my death, this would cause great grief to my mother and make her weep.' She did not say this aloud but her actions indicated this. Lilavati's mother followed the norm of giving similar things to all the three daughters. Lilavati would prevent her mother from giving her anything extra, considering the condition of her in-law's family, and force her to act according to the established norms. While she was ill, her mother would try to follow the norms and make arrangements. Lilavati would prevent her mother from making any expenses for her. She surmised that her end was near and no additional expenses needed to be done for her clothes, etcetera and would not allow her mother to spend on things that she considered unnecessary. But she was cautious that if she were to explicitly state this, her mother would grieve in the present for the impending future; therefore, Lilavati would try and conceal her motive and yet prevent her mother from making such expenses. She employed strategies to ensure that no one noticed her motives. During her long illness, clothes had to be bought for her sister, and her mother would want to buy the same for her as well. Lilavati would usually smile and give a brief response, 'Ba, get anything that you want for the two sisters, don't buy anything for me.' But if she was pressed for an explanation, she would answer, 'Ba, I have become so thin. Anything you buy for me, I will not be able to use them just at present. And when I want to wear them, they would be tight. Therefore, wait for me to get well and put on some weight. And then I will take things according to my taste. So, let us not do anything now.' When she was healthy, she was forced to give up clothes and ornaments because of the circumstances at her in-laws', and, during her illness, she gave these reasons mentioned above for not getting things. But her attitude seemed to change as death approached.

24

The year-long or the year-and-a-quarter-long illness had rendered her so weak that she could barely sit up in the bed. It required great effort. One day, she called her mother and expressed her wish to dress up in fine clothes and ornaments. 'Ba, let us all dress up—you, me, sisters and our sister-in-law. Give me those blue sapphire earrings, give me those necklaces.' She asked for those ornaments and wore them. She insisted others to dress up as well. What was she trying to do when death was so near?

During her moments of 'hysteria', two days later, she blurted out the reason. 'Do you know why I wore all those things? Do you think I really enjoy wearing them or eating everything? All this time I had not worn them and never paid heed to my mother. But now I wore them so that she has no regrets later.'

When she had life in her, she refused these owing to her superior virtues and when death came closer, she wore them moved by deep love, compassion and care for her mother.

One day, her mother's friend visited and told her mother with pain in her heart and tears in her eyes,

Behn, she is a very wise girl. I know a lot of things that she has kept close to her heart. But what am I to do? She has bound me to a promise and said, 'Kaki, be careful, say nothing of this to Ba while I am alive and even after I am dead. If she were to know she would die. Her heart is very delicate. She would not be able to live with this. So, not a word out of you!' Behn! What am I to say about that daughter of yours? Anyway, it's all futile now. Heal the wound of your heart knowing that she was wise.

Lilavati! What you wanted to keep away from your mother must have been something about your penance. It must have ensured fruits in another world. That a daughter of such sterling virtue was born to her is a mark that your mother had earned some merit. God must have destined for you a life in another world that would be ennobling and enriching. Today, either you have attained moksha or obtained an auspicious life. I have endeavoured to fill your mother with such hopes and I extend them to you as an offering. I see that your mother's fiery ordeal has become less severe and that is an appropriate ode to your memory.

Ordinary lives are spent trying to secure personal happiness while alive and efforts to secure the future of our dear ones even after our death. We are moved by egotistical desires during our lifetime and by attachment as we approach death. This is the life of ordinary householders and these colours give hue to their joys and sorrows. The inner scape of Lilavati's heart was differently constructed. During her lifetime, despite compelling reasons, she followed her destiny and tried to live a life of rectitude and duty in each situation. She dealt with all those who came in her contact with affection and a sense of duty. Therefore, her concerns were not about her own self, they were devoid of ego. Whomever destiny and God brought in her contact, she cared for them in a noble way. She strove unceasingly to perform her duties towards them. She would give up an endeavour when action became futile and, with indifference to either success or failure of the effort, she tried to keep away from new cares and desires and in the ultimate instance she was convinced of the goodness of God's authority. These words encapsulate the inner core of Lilavati's heart. Her life was filled with lessons such as these. These embody her sense of duty, her desire for virtues, her noble emotions and her striving, as also her joys and sorrows.

26

We shall try and understand her key to a good and noble life from the point of view of the shastras. The human body and mind follow the rules of physiognomy and psychology without necessarily being aware of them. Most human beings observe the rules of grammar without its awareness, even scholars are not conscious of them in their own literary writing, and yet the rules are followed. Similarly, the hearts and actions of the virtuous by instinct follow norms of good conduct and they are not even aware of their observance. Poet Kalidasa's attention was drawn to this. He says of the virtuous that, when in doubt, be led by your conscience. Evil hearts are drawn to vile actions; similarly, hearts imbued with virtue are attracted to pure, unsullied and righteous actions. In the English language 'conscience' is considered by many scholars as the 'divine voice'. This description applies to persons with virtuous hearts. Such hearts, though not conscious of their own righteous conduct, are pure and noble. Consciousness of religious duty implies awareness of one's duties according to the *dharma shastra* or formulation of righteous conduct through reason. Some human beings are naturally inclined to follow the path of righteousness even without a conscious formulation of rules of conduct. Either as a product of the seeds sown by the ancestors or as a culmination of the good actions of the past births and resultant accumulation of merit or as a combination of these two forces, some fortunate human beings acquire the capacity for instinctual righteous conduct. Some others acquire this capacity through learning as well. Those who consciously follow observations could be led astray by attachment or some other folly, but those who by instinct follow the right conduct are unlikely to deviate from the right path as such conduct is contrary to their nature. The virtue and righteousness that envelop and protect them is devoid of faults. There is an advantage that is available to those who follow norms of duty consciously. They are eager to lead their intellect on the correct path even when it is faced with the obstacles of customs and contingent morality. They also have the means to free themselves of the residue of past actions. We shall at an appropriate stage examine to what extent Lilavati's sense of duty and rectitude was conscious and attained as an endeavour and to what extent her observations were instinctual. What ought to be the pure, conscious sense of rectitude in one such as her, buffeted by the forces of life? How can we surmise that Lilavati's cares and concerns were influenced by sense of religion and duty?

27

What should be the conscious sense of duty? How are we to claim that her concerns and emotions were religious? Oh reader, it is appropriate that you, like Lilavati, should hear it from the discourse of the two characters imagined by this author—Vishnudas and Chandravali. In part IV of *Sarasvatichandra*, Chandravali has spoken about the aspirations of the virtuous. I have not seen anything but such aspirations in Lilavati's heart. In Chapter 25 of the same volume, Vishnudas discoursed on the duties of sacrifice, which Lilavati followed through her observations. Just as a pebble thrown by a child from the top of a mountain by a sea finds the depths of the ocean, similarly, good deeds of a child who occupies a throne reach a vast majority of people. The effects of the actions were widespread because of the high position occupied by the child. Otherwise, his strength was the limited strength of a child's arms. If the same child, instead of being on a mountain top, were to fly a kite from the threshold of his home, the kite would go up only after a great effort. A child born in a poor family can benefit his family only through incessant endeavours. The limited reach of the child is due to his position, otherwise his effort is no different from the one made by a person seated on the throne. Therefore, till we remove the outer layer defined by the placement and condition of a person, we cannot truly compare the observations of a person who occupies a position of weakness. Once we acquire a balanced, unbiased perspective, we must ask how that person followed his eternal duties of sacrifice. Following this perspective, life and world are a great sacrifice, and all human beings occupy one of the three classes therein. There are some persons who feed on others, they seek to fulfil their self-interest through others and they have no care about the pain or happiness of those who sacrifice for them. And even if they were to think about others, moved solely by their self-interest, they do nothing to lessen the burden of others. Those who serve others occupy the position of the initiator of a sacrifice, of a *jajman* in this sacrifice; while those who feed on others are like guests—*atithi*. These 'guests' are persons of lower order, evil and or meek. Those who occupy the middle rung serve others and in turn accept the service of others. When they accept services of others, they become guests and while doing services they become *jajman*. Their offering of sacrifice is not without a purpose, their want is that they should likewise benefit from the sacrifice of others. For them, being a *jajman* is means to an end. The lower order of person only seeks benefit of the sacrifice of others and in no way do they offer services to others. Those who occupy the middle rung are moved by their desires. They do love their sons, but they also desire that their son would serve them in their old age. They want his wife to serve them and fulfil their aspirations. Even if the affection is deep, there is a desire to find a reciprocity for the affection, and when such expectation remains unfulfilled, they become dissatisfied, unhappy and angry with the sons who fail to meet their expectations. Desire begets wrath is a lesson in the Gita and their experience bears testimony to this.

A third class of people are entirely different from these people and they do not wish to be a 'guest' to anyone. They serve the sons and their wives without any expectation of returns, considering them to be guests, and they themselves become host in a detached manner. Either because of the limitation of means, ability or vision they may not be able to do good to others, except their sons and family, but, for them, sons and others are alike. In a crowded train, we make place for a passenger closer to us and not one who stands at a distance; by this same logic, they look after sons and not others but retain equability towards all. Their concerns for their sons and family are their pure, conscious observation of duties. And even if they perform their sacrifice in a detached manner towards the sons, by following the logic of the example of the train, we can consider their sacrifice as complete. Lilavati concluded her sacrifice by her care for those in her natal and marital homes. Given her condition, who could have done more as a host? She fulfilled her duties towards us all and left. This was the conclusion and fulfilment of her obligatory sacrifice.

28

If the lowest kind of human beings do not understand the idea of being a detached, desireless *jajman*, the human beings of the superior order do not know how to be a selfish guest. Every child that is born has the benefits of the boons granted by the parents and place and time in which they live, but those boons are like rain—unsought. Every person is destined to accept such munificence in some form or another. But once intellectual maturity is attained, each person has to decide if she wants to be a host or a guest and also if they wish to act out of desire or in a detached way. This depends on their disposition. The Upanishads say that those in the fourth stage of life—*sanyasa*—should take food for sustenance of the body as one takes medication. Similarly, human beings have to accept the hospitality of others—which is inevitable—like a medicine. *Shruti* describes a Brahminic life even for someone who does not have *yajnopavit*, it also has possibility of *sanyasa* without renunciation. Shastras have described in the same vein a brahmachari who is a householder.

In our times, women did not have the possibility of a life of a celibate ascetic and yet the description of various events will show that Lilavati took the hospitality of her parents and others in very measured way, like medication.

29

Lilavati, though unattached to worldly pleasures, was not devoid of affection. It is affection whenever we are partial to another person. 'Partiality' suggests lack of reason, of thought. How is one to be called a knowledgeable person if one does not have a sense of equanimity towards all? How can such a person be called desireless? In the previous section, we have an example of a passenger giving his seat to another in a crowded train. This is also an instance a partiality.

This partiality is manifested in action, not in the heart. Therefore, we argued that such a person, for this act, does not lose his sense of equability. When such partial actions are righteous and done from a sense of duty, affection that manifests in such action ensure urgency, success and an all-round fulfilment of these deeds. The affection that informs righteous act is itself a form of duty. The same norm that makes Lord Sri Krishna address Arjuna as *sakha* and *priya* also makes the presence of affection in performance of duty appropriate. If a woman were to breastfeed an abandoned child and raise her, it is a conscious act of duty. If this duty is performed with affection, it is even more righteous. It is necessary for a mother to raise her child and feed her with affection for the child's growth and is, to that extent, an instrumental performance of duty. Mother's affection for her child is not cultivated, but when a woman feeds and raises an abandoned child, she reasons 'fate willed that I should be her mother and I see no difference between her and other children'. She follows a conscious duty and her partiality is also righteous. When we disregard this form of affection and recognise only affection and attachment arising out of desire, that person is subject to both attachment and pain. We are often evil to those who are detrimental to the interest of our loved ones. We can free ourselves of false pride but not from attachment and, in the course, do many wrongs moved by affection. Such affection arising out of desire and attachment is common and the example of Gandhari, Dhritrashtra and Kaikeyi is reminiscent of the violation of duty and right conduct for the sake of affection. In such instances, reason becomes subservient to instinct. It is desirable that instinct is subject to reason and affection is subordinate to knowledge and rectitude. We find an embodiment of this in Kaikeyi's son Bharata. Affection towards virtuous, devotion towards teachers, endorsement of the benefit of the company of the virtuous, and compassion towards others are forms of affection and attachment permissible even to the renunciate. Those in other three stages of life can also act with the sense of subtle limits in the exercise of affection. If they are indeed able to do so, they can have detachment and selflessness along with affection in their hearts. Dear reader, it was the good fortune of this author to witness Lilavati's way of being in the world, while remaining detached from it. But this good fortune came and went away too soon. Her mother was both a host and a guest to her and, when she went, her mother wept, 'I have lost my jewel.' Such occasions come in the lives of other parents as well. Other Indian women as daughters, mothers, wives and sisters perform their duty with as much delicacy and subtlety as Lilavati. When I think of them, these living examples of duty embody Saubhagya Devi and Gunasundari—the daughters born out of my imagination. And I look for men in our country capable of such subtle and continuous sacrifice and feel a sense of dejection. Maybe this sense of disappointment is misplaced, but even those men who are exceptions cannot in any way be compared to the atonements scored by women, that which remains unrecognised.

30

The emotions which did not permit Lilavati to accept gifts from her mother at one stage in her life gave way to new sets of emotions as her death approached. Her notion of being a host changed;

awareness of death gave her a different perspective. Her sense of duty forced Lilavati to care and worry for her mother in a variety of ways. She made efforts to provide long-lasting solace to her mother. When she believed that she had a relatively long life, she refused to place any burdens on the resources of her father and, yet, during her illness, she accepted all the expenditure made by her father with a desire to extend her life. When this desire seemed futile and her lifeline appeared diminished, Lilavati recognised the futility of both the efforts and the expenses. But, she did not object to either, only to give solace to her mother. She was committed to speaking the truth, she did not deviate from truth even while striving to assuage her mother's grieving heart. She would ask, like Yaksha,[1] obtuse questions: 'Ba, Mota Kaka spends so much on my medicine, do you think they can fail? Think of it and have patience.' She did not want her mother to mourn after she was gone. She counselled her mother, citing examples from her mother's life:

---

[1] The reference is to the dialogue between Yudhishthira and Yaksha in the Mahabharata.

'Ba, this world is made of pain. If you think that my pain is so great, why do you forget the days of your sorrows?' She would remind her mother of her life's experiences and try to provide a buffer against the destined wound that the mother was fated to receive. She, our ever-loving daughter, thus, became a host to her mother in innumerable ways.

31

Lilavati made a gift of wise counsel and consolation to her mother. She also offered other close relatives what they required and was appropriate.

'Mota Kaka, you gave me so much knowledge. Jasubehn was given some education, but Jayanti got no education. Why did you do that?' Lilavati in form of a polite query admonished me, with regard to one of her sisters.

On another occasion, she expressed her displeasure by saying, 'Mota Kaka, Jasubehn is very naive.'

Lilavati's expression of dissatisfaction and admonishment stemmed from her belief that once it was brought to my notice, I would do something to remedy that. She seized many such opportunities. My response to her would be, 'Lilavati, it is apparent that each one gets according to their destiny. You are learned and Jasu is relatively not but she sings so much better and her handwriting is so good. Jayanti could not study but, compared to the two of you, her in-laws are wealthier.' This answer was not enough for Lilavati. She had not asked those questions to be told about the past, her anxiety was about their future. And for that reason, she repeatedly brought it up. It is not as if naivete cannot be remedied.

Learning gives ability such that intellect is not left unattended and heart does not become subservient to others. She wanted her sisters Jasu and Jayanti to have such abilities. And, at that time, she had greater cause of concern regarding Jayanti who was unlettered. Whenever her mother scolded Jayanti, Lilavati would weep and admonish her mother with tearful eyes. 'Ba! Why do you scold her? Show her the way, point things out to her, this is no way of improving her. Why do you do such things?'

Lilavati, your concern was valid, your reproach was correct. And I had no response to give to you and, for that reason, I gave you only partial answers.

At a time when I educated you, my young heart was filled with enthusiasm and aspirations. Your intellectual development required little efforts, the means for your education and cultivation were easy to obtain and I had enough time for you. My legal practice—which as a sign of good fortune among us—flourished in a short span of time and I had little time to devote to the education of your younger sister Jasvati. When it was time to impart education to Jayanti, I had shifted to Nadiad and could not find appropriate means to educate her. Lilavati! The girls of our country are also sisters to you. The destiny of one of your sisters was like the fate of one type of girls and that of the other was like another group. The fate of one was decided by the active life of your father, and the other one's fate was settled by his decision to retire and live in a village.

Look for the compensation of the harm done to one of your sisters in the good that might have accrued through my actions to others. The harm that I did to Jayanti by not educating her might be compensated by the benefit that our people had from the writing I did during my period of retirement. Now that you are gone, you may not be able to hear my plea to look for other modes of compensation, but you can look at the hearts of your sisters from where you reside. Because you live in their hearts, they live in a distant place but remember you and weep. They seek to follow your example and often say, 'Behn used to do this', 'Behn used to say that'. I have also been told that you gave some advice to their husbands before your death, hoping for an improvement in the fates of your sisters. My clever Lilavati! You gave each according to their capacity to receive. Your gift to your sisters were the words of counsel. I publish this book in the hope that the many sisters of yours in this land may also benefit from it. And in the hope that their husbands become host to them and improve their fates as well.

32

Lilavati, just as you cared for your sisters, you cared for your brother too.

'Mota Kaka, why has Bhai lagged behind? Why did he remain so weak?'

Moti, what am I to do? Even that is his fate. When I came to Nadiad, I felt that he would benefit more if I were to educate him myself and I took him out of the school. You know that soon thereafter I had a long illness and, instead of deriving greater benefit, he was harmed. I couldn't compensate. An attempt to do something good sometimes proves harmful and good comes from something apparently bad. The consequences of a father's action often affect his children. Who is to be held responsible for both good and bad that surfaces? If the father had acted out of self-interest and pride, he is to be held responsible and if he acted out of a sense of duty, then it is fate that is responsible. This answer is both prevalent and familiar in our country. How and with what intentions this author aspired for the welfare of Lilavati and her siblings was well-known to her. Whenever her mother expressed dissatisfaction about her daughter's fate, Lilavati sought to remedy her dissatisfaction and even teased her mother and took her father's side. She counselled her brother. In this instance, her partiality towards me did not permit her to see my fault. Once when I passed by her sickbed, I heard her advise her brother, 'Bhai! Now you have grown up. Do not increase Mota

Kaka's worries, you have to lessen his burden. You must act wisely.'

Lilavati! Was this an expression of concerns for your brother or for your Mota Kaka? What was your advice to your brother? One year after your death, your brother wrote to me in English so that your mother would not be able to read the letter:

> My late learned sister Lilavati is not with me, she is not with you either. But God willed that my heart was once again imbued with love and respect that I had for her. It is quite wondrous and amazing that since last night my sister has been before me, counselling me on matters important for my life. I have stood transfixed listening to her! My eyes brim over with tears as I remember her.

Lilavati, even your brother benefited from your counsel! Your care, concerns, advice, love, your performance of duties, all your subtle riches, all your gifts have stayed with us. The advice you gave your brother from your sickbed could not have been different from the life you led and the duties you performed. Even sinners repent at the hour of their death and gain merit, your faith in the path of rectitude was firm, unmoving and at the last 'station' of your life you counselled your family on matters closest to your heart. This was the duty that you performed, and that duty came to you naturally.

The same sense of duty that made Lilavati care for her mother, sisters and brother, also made her worry about her father, uncle and aunt. Her uncle and aunt had come to Nadiad to serve and nurse her. She wanted them near her during her last days. But her request to her father failed to elicit a response. She has ensured that in the time of her father's retirement he was not required to bear additional expenses. One day, her faith in her father's scholarship to deal with her loss appeared shaken. She called her mother to her bedside and said with astonishment, 'Ba, Mota Kaka addressed me as Behn today.' Her mother replied, 'So what? He must have felt like that.' The daughter replied, 'No, you don't understand. I know that you are fragile but Mota Kaka with his learning would not be feeble. But even he is pained!'

'How do you know that?'

'I looked at his face and body carefully, he looked emaciated!'

'Moti, you have gone crazy. All these medicines have turned your mind soft and hence you feel that others are also weak. What makes you say that he looks weak and withered?'

'Nothing. I shall see to it.'

This was in the morning. At evening, she sat up in her bed and called me. 'Mota Kaka, can we have a discourse?'

'Yes, Behn. Let's discuss what you want.'

'Do, you remember the *Dakshina Murti Stotram*?'

'Yes.'

'Please recite and explain the meaning. I remember it, but at this moment it eludes me. Recite one stanza and explain its meaning. I will also tell you what I make of it and you can correct me.'

'Listen. To Him who sees the universe existing within oneself or like a city seen in a mirror world but appearing externally due to Maya . . . Just as a city's reflection is captured in a mirror, this world is but a form of God and the same supreme God resides in our conscience, the world is but a reflection of Him.'

'Thus, Mota Kaka, all that we see is false, only the God within us is true, isn't it?'

'Yes Behn, exactly. And the verse also gives a reason for this reflection that we see. "It is like a dream existing within oneself." Why do we see a dream when most of our senses are closed? We see that due to the power of sleep. This world, though unreal, appears before us because of the power of Maya. The truth of it lies in the soul of the seer. Just as the dream is not distinct from the dreamer but appears to be such, the world though external is located within oneself.'

Lilavati paraphrased this in her words and asked: 'Is what is said here true?'

'Yes Behn, it is true. The following verse says: 'Who, upon enlightenment, beholds the universe directly as his own non-dual self, salutations unto him'. Shri Dakshina Murti in the form of a master gives us this realisation. One had to stop here and say to her, 'Lilavati, you've exerted yourself enough. You are tired. We shall discuss this further tomorrow. This was some ten–twelve days before her death. She was tired, she needed some peace and rest. She felt tranquil, she felt somewhat rested and asked me to explain *Bhadra Mudra*,[2] which I did and she fell asleep. After sometime, her mother came to me and asked, 'Do you know why she asked you all this?' 'No, what was the reason?' In response, she narrated to me the conversation that Lilavati had with her that morning and said, 'She felt that you have become weak and feeble in the mind. She told me that she would ascertain it herself and for that reason she asked you all of these questions.'

Lilavati! How am to say that your perception was wrong? It was my fate that I should cause you to worry about me even during the last days of your life and so I did that to you. The young have the right to counsel the elderly and in exercise of that right, a daughter awaiting her death counselled her father sound in health. You counselled the father that he should give up his pride. Your questions brought me face to face with truth. And just ten–twelve days before your death, you reminded your father the significance of the *Bhadra Mudra* and opened his eyes. What we call enlightenment came and your father's heart—partial as it is—saw a soft

---

[2] Holding the tip of the forefinger and thumb.

light envelop your body, your face, your eyes. But before my very eyes, the same daughter turned to a corpse, and my fatherhood collapsed. That body—a temple of virtue—remained inert for a while and was soon rushed to the crematorium. My body, now bereft of light, bowed to that temple which people considered lifeless. The sigh 'oh God, oh God' that escaped with great effort was drowned in the sounds of wailing. I willed the tears to stop so that I could have one last darshan of my beloved Lilavati. Our house, unfit to play host to her, became vacant and impoverished. Lilavati, my head bowed to the temple that was your body and, when I lifted my head, that body, that temple had disappeared from my lifeless house. Now all that I can do is remember and venerate your spiritual life. All other sorrows have paled into insignificance and I have a new duty and that is to learn and derive strength from your life and wisdom. Your body is gone but your virtues are before me. Your body has disappeared, but as it is one with God, it is one with me as well.

4

The Flowering

33

Lilavati was born in Nadiad on the second day of the bright fortnight of Chaitra month in Samvat, 1937, which was the 31 March 1881. She died on the fourth day of the dark fortnight of Margshirsha in Samvat, 1958, which was 8 January 1902. Her life ended on that evening. She lived in this world for about twenty–twenty-one years, of which the first two quarters and the last quarter were spent in her father's house, while she lived for a part of it at her in-laws', doing her duties.

What has been described in earlier chapters pertains to the third and fourth parts of her life. This was the time of the development of her mind. It was during this period that her intellect and heart withered due to various fiery ordeals and eventually that tree of life collapsed. We are well acquainted with that. Now we shall acquaint ourselves with that tree of life when it was a seed and a tender sapling.

According to the Western practice, biographies are written in a chronological order of birth, childhood, adolescence and adulthood. But we have adopted a form that is contrary to this and there is a reason for it. Western biographies are life stories of famous men who have performed great deeds in the world. Their exemplary lives are turned into biographies. But many readers are already likely to be acquainted with some parts of these famous lives. And the author presumes that such lives are beneficial to people and that writing of a biography requires no other justification. Hence, believing so, they write a historical account of the life from birth to death.

But the protagonist of our book, Lilavati, had done no remarkable deeds in her life and it is not the purpose of the author to establish that either. A book that is not about a famous hero is better described as a life story rather than as a biography. If it were a biography, it would suffice to say that 'Lilavati lived and her body withered in impoverished condition.' Because she did not have material achievements in this world, Lilavati has nothing to instruct us about that. But this book intends to throw light upon the subtle riches of her character that lay hidden beneath her impoverished state. If the fragrance of this tree has appealed to the reader, the description of its roots and branches is appropriate. So, it is for this reason that the usual form of a biographical narrative has been discarded and the story of her life has been presented in the present form. A person who is attracted to the physical grandeur of a tree examines its roots and trunk and then takes in the fragrance of its flowers and at last the taste of its fruits. But a mind that searches for the subtle senses, takes the fragrance of the flowers in the solitude of his home and looks for the invisible flower that is the source of the fragrance. Only then such a person looks for the tree in the garden. We reversed the order of the life story so that only those refined minds who are attracted by the intangible richness

of this life would read this story right from the roots
of this life.

34

Western biographies begin with the birth of the
subject. But, in order to show the seeds of upbringing
and cultural influences, a short brief on her parents is
given as a preface. Given the fact that this book does
not follow the accepted chronological narrative and
given the relationship of the author of this narrative
with Lilavati, such a section has been considered
inappropriate. There is some reference to the
advice given by her mother through the letters in
the previous section. This gives some idea about the
education and cultivation of her mother. Among us,
there is a belief that samskara of previous birth affects
us and are carried into the next life. This is not the
place to examine the validity of such a belief. The
means to ascertain the presence of such samskara
are also not subject to reasoned examination. But,
when children of the same parents show different
intellect, dispositions, desires and cultivation, the
differences of the samskara of previous birth is

often alluded to. The ground for such assumption is perhaps available in Lilavati's care and concern for her sisters and brother. The fact is that this is too little to make any assumptions about Lilavati's previous life because the education that she received was not made available to her sisters and her brother. Even if we were to accept this limitation, this would not necessarily apply to the period of her life before she began to be educated. When we examine the samskara in the light of her disposition as a mature person, we are inclined to admit that the belief of our shastras in the samskara of previous birth is not without reason. We find examples in support of this in Lilavati's life and in each and every household. Among us, people of all classes believe to some extent in astrology. If there be any truth to this shastra, a person takes rebirth to fulfil the deeds of the previous births and also gets the fruits of such previous acts. Lilavati's mother would show her and her sisters' birth charts to many astrologers and Lilavati would carefully listen to the readings thus made. Such readings have in some cases been wrong and, in some cases, have been right. The description of Lilavati's intellect and such likes has proved to be correct, to some extent also wrong. Prompted by curiosity to ascertain what of it proved correct, the author found the following, which begs consideration.

Mars in the 8th place [in her birth chart] makes a woman ample, full of love for her husband, but weak in spirit.

She tends to be always favourable, devoted to religious rituals, endowed with an adorable body as well as excellent qualities that she could be proud of.

Venus [Shukra] when properly placed [in the birth chart] of the girl makes her pious [*dharmapara*] and with a pleasant face behaving as she should [*vihitam*]. The dark one [Raahu] which moves easily [swift] makes a woman somewhat lacking in happiness, always overwhelmed, suffering from eye ailments, capable of giving birth to a moderate number of children, devoted to duties of gift making, of a happy contented temperament and enjoying connection to good persons.

If we were to read this without any pride or prejudice, it contains the essence of her life story and with that we can conclude the discussion about the samskara of the previous births. The belief of the author that his daughter's samskara were of the kind that have been described finds affirmation from the fact that she forever declined to accept any physical luxuries and money that the author sought to provide for her and this also allows the author to realise, at the cost of his pride, that the learning and knowledge she had received were his daughter's own capabilities and were not given to her by anyone. Quite contrary to his proposition, Lilavati was ever grateful to her parents for the education that they provided and did not attribute her learning either to her samskara or her good faith, and yet, at the same time, she did not blame anyone for her pain and suffering but attributed it to her fate and sought solace in that. When Shakuntala realised that the amnesia of her husband was due to a curse she had received from a sage, she harboured no ill will or bitterness towards him and her heart gained peace and equanimity. Similar peace and equanimity permeated Lilavati's heart at a time when she was engulfed by troubles and disease. The reason for this was her inclination to see her own destiny responsible for this. We have seen that she had no ill will towards anyone either at her in-laws' or her parental home. Despite the shortcomings in the hospitality and, while bearing the burdens of such imperfect hospitality, she was ever grateful to all those who were 'host' to her. This is one of the characteristics of the virtuous—that they see no fault in others but only the goodness in all their acts. Lilavati had obtained this quality either as a reward from her actions in her past life or this was something that was innate in her since birth.

35

Now we shall describe as to how Lilavati was tutored in household matters and educated in letters. This author began his legal practice in the city of Bombay in 1884. At that time, there was a girl's school quite adjacent to a relative's home in Zaver Baug. In fact, the school could be seen from the window of this house. This was the house of the author's youngest sister, the late Samarthlaxmi and her husband Changanlal Harilal Pandya BA. Lilavati was initially admitted to this girl's school. During recess, she would go to her dear aunt's house and play and, while she was at the school, we could see her activities from the house. In a short time, we changed house and all of us moved across the main road in an area called Malharrao's wadi. As Ra. Changanlal was a government servant, he obtained a job in the State of Junagadh and moved there. Lilavati previously had enjoyed the benefit of her aunt's presence, which was now lost. Her father's heart did not feel at peace in letting her go to the school by crossing the main road and being alone in the school for five to six hours. This main road has incessant movement of trams, horse-drawn carriages and people going about their work. It is natural to be scared while sending a child across such roads unaccompanied.

Lilavati had her aunt's place to go to during recess or when she was uncomfortable at school; but that too was no longer available. Her father did not have the means to retain a servant who would accompany her to school and wait through the day. Moreover, in those times, for girls of her age, school education was more play than actual learning. Lilavati was still a child and, truly speaking, it was not proper to burden her with studies. There were no other girls' schools nearby. Considering all this, she was taken out of the school after some months. She was not admitted to any other school and, as per her age, sex and body, arrangements were made at home for her play and fun. This would also point out that the thoughts and considerations similar to mine have become obstacles between our girls and the portals of girls' schools.

36

Some three–four years passed by. Lilavati was growing up. The decision to not send her to school remained and added to that was the need to provide her training in household matters, which could be best given at home. How long do our girls have to study? Only till such time that they are made to go to their in-laws'! Whatever nurturance one needs for their intellect must be given in this period. It is futile to hope for any intellectual nurturance after that. Only their husbands can become their gardeners and nourish their intellect thereafter. But, quite often, the husbands are incapable of nurturing them. And even if they are capable, they have other obstacles to cross, quite often their families become a hurdle or their own need to earn a livelihood does not give them enough opportunity or the young brides engaged in household chores do not have the scope to develop their intellect. If all the other conditions are favourable, sometimes their intellect is dull or they hear questions like 'what has a girl to do with education?' and are frightened by the ignominy that comes with education, many such fears arise and women remain devoid of education and learning remains distant from them. When Lilavati was ten years of age, her father felt that before such obstacles arise in the path of learning, the foundation of her knowledge must be built so that she could ably use that knowledge in her later years. In the early sections of this book, there are some examples of questions posed by the little Lilavati, some other such questions made this resolve firm. 'A short night and many acts' is a saying among us. The difficult question was—how broad and solid an education could be provided to her in such a short time that she had. It was not for me to create opportunities for this intelligent girl to live an unmarried life, given our customs. But God filled her father's heart with a desire to give her such knowledge that she could live happily at her in-laws'.

37

It is not possible to give our daughters knowledge through our girls' schools. School education consists only of rudimentary reading and writing and some elementary arithmetic. For those who cannot obtain even this much at home, this education suffices but we gave up the idea of sending her to a school with the conviction that we would be able to give her much more at home. We began her education in Gujarati at home when she was about eight or nine years old. We began as it is our custom with the alphabet and soon she was able to read. Her teacher was told to teach her mathematics that would enable her to make calculations for the household finances. Along with this education, her mother taught her household skills. It is proper for our daughters to learn these skills from their mothers, because, in this training, affection, tenderness and even the right to give punishment are required and, in all this, there is not one who has greater trust of our daughters than their mothers. Once the daughter leaves her mother's side, the hope to learn these skills as and when responsibilities come her way or be taught by her in-laws is quite futile and often results in strife.

In a short time, Lilavati acquired elementary knowledge and skills in both these domains and a routine was fixed for her. Cooking requires both stamina and long practice. Therefore, from the age of eleven–twelve she was given the responsibility of cooking for the family. Her mother was told not to interfere in her cooking, so that before she went to the in-laws' house, she would be able to cook for a family of twelve or thirteen persons. This would take up till mid-day. Everyone was instructed not to assign any household work to Lilavati for the rest of the day, nor was she allowed to contribute to household work beyond this. The remaining part of the day and early hours of night were to be devoted to her studies.

For some time, she studied in the evening with a teacher—Bhandarkar's Sanskrit *Margopadesika* and the first book of English. During the day, she read Gujarati books, embroidered, rested and played. This went on for some days. I had been looking for a gentleman who could teach her Sanskrit and classical knowledge. Her teacher introduced me to Shastri Jivram Lallubhai. Shastriji had obtained a degree of Acharya from a *peetha* at Kashi and was learned in grammar and other shastras. He was new to Bombay and, since he had no acquaintances in the city, he was quite reserved. As we became aware of his scholarship, first Lilavati and then her mother, both became his students. From time to time we set new targets in their learning, which he fulfilled.

Sanskrit grammar is limitless and unfathomable and even elementary knowledge requires a lot of time, and Lilavati had little time for studies and much to learn. Lilavati had no use for the ability to compose in this great language, therefore, she was required to be taught enough Sanskrit so that she could read and infer its meaning without any help. A child learns a new language without the aid of a book, just by practice. And travellers likewise learn a foreign language. Shastriji adopted the same method and did not use any books, save some elementary works. Apart from learning grammar, Lilavati had to expand her vocabulary. She was given *Amar Sara* and another Sanskrit–Gujarati dictionary for self-study. Shastriji also used the *Amar Sara* to expand her knowledge of words. There was need to introduce her to Sanskrit literature, but there was an obstacle in this as there were usually parts with *sringara* in them. It was decided that *sringara* need not be taught to her and these parts were omitted and rest of the text was taught. She was taught Bhartrihari's *Niti Sataka*, *The Cand-Kaushika of Arya Ksemisvara*, the fourth part of *Abhijnana Shakuntala* and third act of *Uttar Rama Charitra*. This enabled Lilavati to obtain enough knowledge from this language to study Sanskrit books without the guidance of a teacher. In her spare time, she read the remaining parts of *Shakuntala* and *Savitri Nataka* with the aid of a dictionary and commentaries. She sometimes asked Shastriji to resolve her queries. The knowledge that she acquired through this method did not enable her to answer questions of our university examinations, but the great outcome of such literary training is that it fills the heart with noble emotions and aspirations, it pushes out lowly passions and imbues the heart with higher aspirations. Lilavati's heart, like a hive filled with honey, imbibed these aspirations; but the test of it should be left to you, dear reader.

38

She has just begun to dip into the first two 'Readers' of English. At that time, Lilavati's study of Sanskrit expanded and with that her love for that language. As a result, she turned away from English education. How was one, trained on *Shakuntala* and *Uttar Rama Charitra*, to find 'reading books'—of modern kind for children—interesting? The reason for starting her off on English education was that if her husband wanted her to study English and he was ready to provide assistance to Lilavati in this regard, she would be equipped and this introductory education would ease her path. At that time, it was felt that she had acquired elementary knowledge and according to her wishes English education was dropped. Thus, now she could now spend all her time in the subjects that she liked. She used this opportunity to enhance her classical learning. Study of literature creates high aspirations and superior aesthetic sensibility but the tender creeper-like intellect requires the support of the shastras to grow. No other shastra can provide the pure and exacting intellectual exercise like logic does. A study of logic chisels every aspect of the intellect from each side, and provides a framework for comparative analysis of significance of things. Motivated by this idea, this author requested Shastriji to teach Lilavati *Laghu Tark Kaumudi*.[1]

If logic is an intellectual exercise of the mind, in our community, from times immemorial, intellect has been regarded as a part of the attainment of spiritual accomplishment and this is as it should be. This shastra provides such a protective shield to the heart that the suffering the world does not pierce it. Thus, our sages have given to us the gift of the shastras that work for this worldly as well as the other worldly aspirations. The author felt that Lilavati should not be deprived of the benefits of

---

[1] Also known as *Laghu Siddhanta Kaumudi*. An abridgement of Bhattoji Dikshita's *Siddhanta Kaumudi*, a text on Panani's grammar.

this learning and accordingly suggestions in this regard were made to Shastriji who enthusiastically accepted them. Shastriji taught Lilavati *Panchikaran*, Isa and Ken Upanishads with some commentaries and Bhagavad Gita with commentary appropriate for her age and intellect. Her intellect, yet not mature enough, did find these subjects demanding but she was deeply interested in them. She read on her own *stotras* from compilations like *Stotra Kalap* and, when the meaning appeared too obtuse, she sought Shastriji's help. Her intellect and heart benefited from the study of *Nyaya Shastra* and Vedanta, and these gave her the strength to pass through very trying circumstances. The author has tried to narrate, for the benefit of the reader, some of these aspects. Just as the movement of the hand aids walking, study of *Nyaya Shastra* provides subtle strength in the search for the divine and aids progress. Just as logic by itself is lame, faith alone is blind, the coming together of both the shastras is necessary to pass through this world. It is appropriate that the reader should judge how the two shastras gave strength and faith to her heart and the manner in which it aided her intellect.

Knowledge of Sanskrit in this country is beneficial to both men and women but, in this age, it is likely to be one-dimensional, and an intellect satisfied only with that is likely to be weak like a blind person guided only by sound. This disability can be countered by a combination of Sanskrit and Western learning. As described earlier, since Lilavati had developed a distaste for English, there was only one way of combining the two types of knowledge. 'Reading books' to acquire knowledge of English, we have very limited resources available in Gujarati that can acquaint one to the vastness of English learning. This paucity was even more acute ten to twelve years ago. In order to provide Lilavati some knowledge in our tongue, I placed in her hands Karsandas Mulji's *England Ma Pravas*, the daily *Gujarati*, and some other periodicals along with the other books that she asked for. On one side, she chose this path and, on the other, she read Bholanath Sarabhai's *Prarthana Mala* and also read *Bhamini Bhushan*.

It is often asked, what girls and women should read, a similar question had bothered this author while getting books for Lilavati and his answer to it was as above. Means of knowledge have both nectar and poison, what proves to be nectar for one sex or one person often proves poison to another and vice versa. It is the responsibility of the parents of our daughters to determine, based on the consideration of the intellect of the girl and her future, which would be nectar and which would be poison. But, it is absolutely certain that to keep our daughters unlettered is to deny them destiny; not just that but there are no better means than good education to guide her on the correct path and enable her to choose an engagement when she is idle. When it is impossible for her to have a friend who is like-minded and who shares her tastes, she cannot be allowed to feel orphaned and not even parents or other women have the capacity to give her strength to point to her the path of rectitude. And in the dark night that the world is, the protection of girls from the cold that chills them is given by the light that guides them through the unlit paths on which they stumble and the warmth that they obtain from good knowledge. This is unmatched by all other means. If such empowering quality lies in the shastras, in our times proximity to Western learning also has power to illuminate. In the short time available at the paternal home, such proximity cannot be provided. Our girls' schools provides only a glimpse of knowledge that is akin to the gazing at the stars from earth. If there is anyone who can provide such proximity to knowledge to a girl, it is her husband and there are many obstacles that hover above him. In our society, there are many hardships in the path of women should they wish to acquire fuller appreciation of knowledge. And yet it is possible for our daughters to obtain through their own efforts, books and newspapers in our language. They contain many subjects both beneficial and harmful. And if she were to, using her intellect over which she has some control, to think independently about the beneficial aspects of knowledge, her perspective is likely to expand and find a place in her heart. Lilavati in her life found this ring true; if she faced hardships with solace derived from the shastras, she dealt with setbacks without feeling orphaned and lonely with the knowledge that she had, which pointed to her the paths of hope and rectitude.

40

Even those, who accept that Western knowledge is useful for those girls who have access to Sanskrit learning would question that if Sanskrit knowledge could be secured, would it not be sufficient for the mental development of girls and can they not do without other forms of knowledge? There is a saying amongst us that 'a life of observation is better than life of having not seen anything at all'. This is not said in the praise of purposeless curiosity of the human mind but it contains a high principle of human cultivation. The same principle is to some extent involved in giving some fragments of Western education to girls. Men and women who have travelled are more experienced, clever, generous and forgiving than those cooped up in the house. The English poet Shakespeare says: 'Home keeping youths have ever homely wits.'[2] This has been said about those men and women who through their travel have broadened their intellect and other qualities. Among us it is usually said: 'The one who

---

[2] *The Two Gentlemen of Verona*, Act 1, scene 1.

travels to different countries and remains in service of a learned person experiences his intellect expand like a drop of oil on water. Those who neither travel nor apprentice with the learned have their intellect contract like a drop of ghee on water.' It is also said that travel provides the opportunity to visit holy places, make wide acquaintances, earn wealth, observe wonders and acquire cleverness of intellect and refinement of language. These sayings usually apply to men but if we were to think carefully, it would become apparent that they are equally true for women.

Just as pilgrimage has been considered beneficial for men, it also is for women. Not only that, but, according to the Hindu code, a woman who is dependent upon a man for her needs ought to be provided not only food and adequate clothing but, depending upon the availability of means, provisions for her pilgrimage also need to be made. Thus, the benefits of pilgrimage and travel are available to women just as men. The other benefit of travel is the possibility of making wide acquaintance, which even the women acquire within the limits demarcated by right conduct. The third benefit is acquisition of wealth, which does not apply to women but given our time and context, considering it totally irrelevant would not be possible. Among the wealthy, the women of the family, in absence of male members, often shoulder the responsibility of looking after and even augmenting wealth. Among such women, the life of Harkuvar Sethani[3] of Ahmedabad is well known. She was of course extremely wealthy but even other women have to deal with money depending upon their context and circumstances. If not for earning money then for preservation and protection of wealth, women have undertaken travels, and many such examples of Nagar women can be cited from about twenty-five years ago. In those days, women belonging to families of landowners or families that held high positions in the administration of native states used to ride horses to travel. There is no reason to believe

[3] After the death of her husband, Hutheesing Kesarising, Harkuvar Sethani managed the business and supervised the construction of a large Jain shrine, called *Hutheesing Nu Derasar*, in 1848, the cost of construction was Rs 12 lakh at that time. She also endowed schools for girls and a teacher's training institute specifically to train teachers for the schools for girls.

that givers of our shastras have reserved the right to travel and garner knowledge from it only for the men and have forbidden women, who are naturally more curious than men, from travelling.

Places of pilgrimage span the length of the country from the Himalayas to Setubandh Rameshwar. These places are in naturally beautiful terrain and have many attractions. To assume that women should not witness the beauty of these wondrous places is to place a false charge upon the givers of the shastras. Pilgrimage makes the intellect sharper and language refined, both of which apply to men and women alike. Women of our country are not to be caught up in the shackles of household work and responsibilities forever and must be freed from these and taken as partners, as much as possible. Thus, the sages have shown pilgrimage to be beneficial for women and have given the men the responsibility to make this possible. In our times, either due to paucity of funds or miserliness, pilgrimages have become fewer but it is possible to provide the benefits of travel by acquainting women with the appropriate knowledge. We began this section with this proposition and in the following section we shall explicate upon them.

41

The earlier section considers travel as one of the means of broadening the intellect, the same verse describes the benefits of apprenticeship to a learned person. The apprenticeship to a man of learning is obtained both by proximity to such a person as also by reading superior books. Just as travel provides knowledge about sacred places, so does books on travel. The Sanskrit word *tirtha* has two meanings: sacred and beautiful places and learned and virtuous sages. The elders of the family are akin to *tirtha*, the same is true for the elders of this land. Just as travel brings us closer to both kinds of *tirtha*—physical as well as spiritual—similarly, geography, travelogues and study of material world brings knowledge of the physical world and study of history and biographies bring us closer to the lives of the virtuous. We must remember how Sitaji was shown paintings of the forest to cultivate in her a desire for life in the forest. *Uttar Ram*

Charitra describes that the wives of seers travelled to the abodes of the learned great souls to obtain knowledge. Pilgrimage to sacred places is being in the proximity of places and persons of virtue; remembering these virtues and singing praises of them is one mode of observation and study which can be obtained by books. Travel brings us knowledge of *tirtha* and also acquaints us with both good and bad aspects of things and persons, this makes an educated person worldly-wise and not remain confined to bookish knowledge but, instead, helps them acquire practical knowledge.

In the ancient times, education of women comprised music, painting and reading histories of both good and bad men; this would not escape the memory of those who have read the *Kama Shastra*, *Malati–Madhav* and *Kadambari*. The benefits that accrue through travel are often made available to our women through the study of diverse books. To keep them naive or stupid, to keep them aloof from the high and the low currents of society and keep them ignorant of practical matters, which also requires discernment of virtue, is to keep them unprotected. If we were to adopt such a path for women who are the light of our households, they would tremble at each gust of wind and their lights would be extinguished. Such a path has not been advocated, it has not been considered a desirable path; those who are curious about it need to be reminded of the worldly wisdom and learning of Draupadi that is evident through many dialogues of the Mahabharata and the poem *Kirata–Arjun*. The necessity and the benefit of educating women and their capabilities are evident in the examples of Sati Chuni Gauri,[4] who rescued the family of Desaiji of Bharuch and the queen Ahalyabai who ably ruled over the kingdom of Indore. It has been considered a duty to provide all women—even with limitations of means and context—similar education. The attempt has been to establish this imperative. We have dealt with only two aspects of the process by which the intellect is broadened. The other aspects have not been included and elaborated here because their need and desirability would be established by the foregoing discussion.

---

[4] G.M.T. wrote a story in English on the life of Chuni Gauri, called *Chuni, the Sati*.

We have come in contact with a Western ruler. Hence, under such circumstances, it is essential to prepare our women for all its consequences; we should consider Western learning akin to travelling, and their welfare and our security lies in making that knowledge available to them. This is in accordance with the norms set up by the ancient Indians. One illustration should suffice to exemplify this notion of welfare and harm. At present, there is a deadly plague epidemic sweeping across our land. It is imperative to stay away from the diseased and seek safety at a distance from the areas that have come under the grip of the disease. This is known to both the young and the old in the Western continent. Our shastras say that those who inhabit such forbidden places are to be eaten by a rakshasi named Vishuchika. It is the boon that was granted to her by Brahma. Thus, what is known to the Western world, which is half the world, and known to our shastras is not known to men living in our countryside and villages and it is quite natural that is not known to their women as well. People living in large cities like Bombay and big towns know this fact more than people living in villages. As a result, when an epidemic hit, people in the cities found better safety while people in villages and towns perished. In a city like Bombay, with a population of nine lakhs, during the peak of the epidemic, there were about 300–400 deaths; by that logic, in a city with one lakh people, the number of death should be between thirty-three to thirty-four, and in a town of 30,000, the deaths should not exceed twelve to fifteen. While in Surat, with a population of one lakh, there have been about hundred deaths per day and towns with population of 30,000 have reported about forty deaths. Thus, Surat has three times the death of Bombay and a town with 30,000 persons counted about nine times more deaths than that of Bombay. And in smaller villages, the ratio is likely to be much higher. The reason for this is the orphaned and destitute condition and the illiteracy of the people in the villages. In small villages, both men and women are similarly illiterate, while in towns where men are literate either because they have received Western education or because they have come into contact with Western modes, women continue to suffer illiteracy and, in times of epidemic, women do not have the courage to do what is required of them. If the woman is not ready to come out and leave the house, our culture does not allow men to force them to do otherwise. I have heard and seen many such stories about women obstinately refusing to leave their homes and succumbing to the disease, and we shall continue to hear of such things in the future as well. Women from cities like Bombay have some protection against such illiteracy by association with the literate and among others; this is a factor that contributes to the low fatality rate from the disease there. The minimum knowledge that women in cities acquire just through association can be provided elsewhere through instructional books and books on Western knowledge. If this could be done, the intensity of the disease could be countered to some extent. This country had borne the brunt of this disease for the past seven to eight years.

But there are other instances of illiteracy as well. The pallus—*stree-dhan*—of women are mismanaged either by their relatives or moneylenders. If women were to know about the boon and protection of 'saving banks', they could be protected to a large extent. Among us, women from communities of ironsmiths, metal workers and goldsmiths assist their husbands and sons in their work, in Europe, women of mercantile class and wives of writers help their husband's work. Similarly, if women of Brahmin and Vaisya communities were to receive education about trade and practical affairs, the wealth of their families would increase and also be protected. The history of the world is well-acquainted with the means to be adopted and the expected results of such efforts. Among us, we can see its impact and experience will bear this out. There is only one way to obtain this result. Our women are completely devoid of Western cultivation and this is not how it should be. Each one, depending upon their capacity and intellect, should get women to walk the path of Western learning. This subject can be expanded further by many illustrations but it would be proper to conclude this discussion. If we can help our women to travel this path outlined above, we can secure the benefits of their intellectual expansion for our age. This would lead to the welfare of the women as well as the entire society. That it is the duty of Indian men to ensure this, has been well established by the foregoing discussion.

42

Our people believe that Western education alone is poisonous for our girls and creates obstacles and problems for their relatives. This belief is not entirely baseless, without foundation or untrue. However, the fault is not of Western knowledge but of the pedagogy of that education. Poison administered with proper knowledge is like nectar and nectar administered inappropriately works like poison. This is not the place to discuss the pedagogy of Western education for our girls. We will try and answer it in one or two brief sentences.

It suffices to say that it should be such that poison can be kept out and they receive only nectar. Sanskrit knowledge is like a mother's milk for the children of this country and, for this very reason, it is easily digestible and provides protection and nurturance throughout life. If we were to fly our kite in the sky of Western learning, whose orientation and values are different, and if this kite is not attached to this land though strong threads, it is likely to cause some disorder. Before we send out our kite-like daughters to fly in that sky, we should take these precautions as kite fliers, and if we are cautious and clever about it this, the knowledge imparted becomes the harmless nectar. Lilavati was not given that education but was exposed to its fragrances as discussed in section 39. These fragrances and aroma, like *kasturi*, permeated through her heart. This we shall describe when the occasion presents itself. She did not attend a school and for this reason she was never at a distance from the values of the family. She was exposed to the flavours of Western knowledge in the environment of the family and, in section 35, we have described how she was taught household skills. She was also introduced to Sanskrit literature and shastras. This author's heart knows well how beneficial her familiarisation with Western learning was. The beneficial aspects were in the practical domain and for this reason they are not included at length in this life story. We shall narrate and illustrate the influence of this learning on her conduct and words at appropriate places. But how is the author, who cannot find any fault with her, even begin an evaluation of its impact? If this author has succeeded in his attempt to convey the reasons for which he exposed Lilavati, who was as tender as a plant, to the wind of Western learning, the purpose of this chapter may be regarded as fulfilled.

5

Affective Universe

43

A seed grows and is transformed into a tree with many branches, covered in its own foliage and laden with flowers and fruits. A child with tiny limbs grows to become a mature person strong in body. A child evolves from a stage of innocence and instinct to become a person with intellect, desires and emotions, which forms the world of that person, sometimes high and sometimes low. The life of a householder is the first of many such steps and, even on that initial step, one is filled with ideas, desires and emotions.

Ordinary persons have desires untampered with emotions, the middle rung is occupied by persons who have both desires and also emotions, while the finest people have emotions untainted by desires. Intellect becomes an instrument of either desires or emotions, whichever is stronger. We have seen how Lilavati's conduct towards all members of the family was devoid of desire. Emotions untainted by desires are superior to those which are laced with passions. We shall try and illustrate the form that it took in Lilavati.

44

Love or affection is also an emotion. One day, Lilavati's mother scolded Lilavati's child for some reason. The child was about two years of age. Lilavati, diseased and confined to her bed, heard the scolding and thought it to be inappropriate. But she did not say anything or intervene until her mother came to her bedside. And then, ever so softly, she said, 'Ba, nothing will come out of scolding him. You cajole him, get him to do what you want playfully, he will learn something from that and you too will have it your way.' To that, her mother responded, 'You are adept and clever with your ways, I am not.' Lilavati did not press the point any further. Whenever her mother scolded her younger sister Jayanti, Lilavati, moved by affection for her sister, would weep and say, 'What is one to say to Ba? Jayanti is at fault but I cannot bear Ba scolding her.'

What was unbearable in case of her sisters became something she could endure in case of her child. Because she knew that a grandmother's love is in no way less than a mother's love. In case of her sister, Lilavati could see the injustice in her mother's excrcise of customary authority. If she found this unacceptable, she also found her sister's folly equally troubling.

Once Lilavati and her mother sat talking on the swing. She blurted out, 'Ba, you do not know how to uphold Mota Kaka's prestige! Do you even know the high regard with which he is held in the society?' I overheard the conversation and I went up to them and asked her, 'Lilavati, what did you say to your mother?' She repeated her statement, to which I said, 'Moti, it is better that your mother remains unconcerned about such reputation.' Lilavati did not respond. She had some measure of that artificial fame from reading newspapers and journals, but she could immediately see that her mother was untouched by those journals and any talk of my reputation could only create barriers between the two of us, which was undesirable. These are some examples of what Lilavati wanted her mother's mental universe to be.

45

If Lilavati had aspirations about her mother, she had ideas about what she wanted her father to be like. Lilavati was about fourteen or fifteen years of age. At some festival, someone told her, 'Lilavati, your Mota Kaka is considered an atheist in the world outside.' Lilavati was more concerned about how I really was rather than what the world thought about me. She asked her mother, 'Ba, is Mota Kaka an atheist?' She was not satisfied with the answer and for that reason she came up to me and asked in a somber but eager voice, 'Mota Kaka, is this really true?' I did not give a straight answer and instead asked, 'What do you think?' She replied, 'I believe that my Mota Kaka cannot be an atheist.' To that I said, 'That is enough. What you know to be true must be so.'

During her final days of illness, she had a doubt about something else. The fourth part of *Sarasvatichandra* was nearly printed, but I had to keep the fates of my protagonists unknown even to my family. There was much speculation about the eventual resolution of the novel and Lilavati had heard some of these as well. One day, as she lay in her sickbed, she asked me in a grave voice, 'Mota Kaka, what have you intended for Kumud?'[1]

'Behn, I cannot disclose that to anyone.'

'Why not?'

'First, because only I can provide the answer and I alone cannot match the curiosity of the countless persons who ask the question. The second reason is that until I wrote the concluding chapters, even I did not know how I would bring about a resolution.'

---

[1] Kumud, the female protagonist of *Sarasvatichandra*, was a widow. The speculation was about her possible remarriage to the male protagonist Sarasvatichandra.

'But you have completed the novel, haven't you? You must know her fate now.'

'Yes, I do. But my response to all those who ask this has been that I cannot reveal the end, and I would be a liar if I told you and not the others, and for that reason even your curiosity shall remain unresolved.'

She raised her eyebrows and spoke in a tone of authority. 'All that is fine. Let me say this to you plainly—you shall not allow Kumud to remarry. You may do anything else.'

Behn! Lilavati! Your concern for me was like that of my mother. My righteous and God-fearing father desired that I should follow the path of devotion and rectitude more than he desired for me a life of riches. You, too, had adopted these virtues and affection which made you partial towards me and did not permit you to see any folly in me. The mere possibility of a failure of mine made your heart tremble with fear. Lilavati! Your concern for me was like that of my parents towards me, you cultivated similar aspirations for me. The wish that you had expressed from your deathbed was like a command from my parents, which had to be obeyed. If my conclusion had been different from what you had desired, I would have been compelled to change the conclusion in obedience to your desire, it would have given rise to a tumultuous conflict within me— whether I should follow what my heart desired and what seemed to secure the welfare of the country or change the conclusion to what you wanted it to be. It was my good fortune that I could respond to you with a smile: 'Behn, you should not worry on that count.' I was not required to go against your affectionate care for your father and did not also have to struggle with my heart.

My heart, ever partial to Lilavati, did not see any fault in her, similarly, she believed and hoped that her parents too were free of follies, and that they were capable of fulfilling the aspirations that she harboured for them. Her feelings on this aspect remained intense throughout her life.

46

In ordinary parlance and behaviour, 'devotion' implies faith or reverence towards a person or God. Devotion to one's mother implies that one sees no fault in her and reverence allows for only the virtues to come to mind. There is a saying that one should not judge the character of one's elders. It is likely that one might find a flaw in their character which could result in lesser reverence for them, which is undesirable from the perspective of children who love them. Therefore, one should at any mention of the character of the elders close one's ears and neither hear, speak nor think about it. Such thoughts arise from the generous disposition of children and not from their discerning minds. In our contemporary society, in certain situations, we need generosity more than we need discerning intellect and for that reason it is appropriate that such ideas are widely shared.

But Lilavati's notions differed from this. She did not think it necessary to turn deaf, mute and blind to her parent's flaws. She did not also believe that doing so was a sign of right conduct and duty. Saint poet Narsinh Mehta has said:

> *Desert all that come between*
> *You and Narayan*
> *Desert the wealth, the body,*

The loved ones and home,
Prahlad deserted his father,
But held steadfast to Hari-Naama,
Bharat-Shatrughana deserted their mother
But not the worship of Rama.[2]

We will try and answer it in one or two brief
sentences. In section 10, we acquainted ourselves
with the principle that Lilavati had formed as a guide
to her conduct: 'It is a duty to follow the commands
of elders but God is supreme among elders and one
is not to follow any injunctions of parents or any
other elders if it is in violation of the command of
God.' She had also formed a view of her parents.
She believed that notwithstanding the condition
of the society around her, the lives of her parents
were moral and unsullied and they had no faults for
which she should be ashamed. It is unnecessary to
speculate how she would have coped with our faults
or how she would have followed the injunctions of
the saint poet and how pained she would have been

---

[2] Translated by Prathistha Pandya from the original Gujarati for
this work.

at our moral turpitude. It is both out of place and inappropriate, at least for this author, to evaluate whether her belief in the purity of her parents was founded in truth or a result of her affection for her parents. For the present, our intent is to know what lay in Lilavati's heart. An attempt has been made to demonstrate that the principles that abided in her heart were not an illusory web of words but the very breath of her life. In section 12, we saw that she had cried out: 'But who was the one to utter such harsh words? My mother—one who has been educated by you, the one who taught me my duties towards my mother-in-law. That very mother said such words! How am I to bear this?' She saw that her mother, the source of her affective universe, had wavered from her teachings and the tears that flowed were meant to cleanse the layer of impurity that had come to sully her mother's emotions. The male sensibility of the saint poet had sought renunciation, while the delicate but hopeful power of the female heart churned her mother's inner core and stymied the folly that had begun to take root and grow.

We have described in the previous two sections how she was compelled to express her feelings whenever she suspected that her parents were about to deviate from the highest norms that she expected of them. She would command her parents to remain at the highest peak of moral conduct. It is not out of place to mention in one line what authority she brought to bear through her pious commands and other modes through which she sought obedience from us.

When she inquired about the fate of Kumud in the fourth part of *Sarasvatichandra*, this author had posed a counter question to her: 'Lilavati, in your view, what would be Kumud's fate?' She promptly replied, 'I am convinced that she would live and reform Pramaddhan.'[3]

The authority and tact with which Kumud could have possibly reformed Pramaddhan were similar to those adopted by intelligent and pious daughters to reform their elders. If we accept that this was in Lilavati's heart, we get one key to enter it. It is true that other considerations prevailed and Lilavati's expectations regarding Kumud were not met in the novel. But it is also true that such a conclusion was

---

[3] In section 3 of the novel, Kumud had drowned and been given up for dead. Pramaddhan was her debauched husband.

contemplated by the author who had even written such an eventuality, but since it contradicted the design and flow of the novel, it was abandoned.

<h2 style="text-align:center">47</h2>

We have seen through many examples how Lilavati viewed her parents, what her aspirations were for them and the state of her emotions as she navigated through the social world that she was a part of. We shall try and remove the layers of examples and examine her universe within.

The expectations and desires of our average women are about food and drinks, clothes and ornaments, the affection and respect of the family and also towards garnering prestige among the members of the caste, the village or the city. Even virtuous women participate in these activities to aid the prosperity of their husbands. Under such circumstances, and despite possessing all means, the ability to exercise restraint in consumption is a form of penance. Women who seek delight in possessions and their consumption does not allow them to care for their families adequately and, for such reasons, sage

Kanva advised Shakuntala to be 'not elated with pride in prosperity.'[4] Lilavati had been taught that part of *Shakuntala*, as she conducted herself in keeping with that advice. This need not be emphasised for the reader of this tale. What she consumed and enjoyed even within limits were not without a reason. We have described her attitude towards clothes and ornaments, and shown the reasons for which she showed restraint in using even what she had. But we have hitherto not discussed reasons for which she used what she did. One day, a discussion about this arose. She said, 'Mota Kaka, I should wear finery so that no one has a chance to speak ill of you.' She said to her mother, 'I do not need to wear anything in excess of that.' She had this rule for herself, but was very enthusiastic about acquiring clothes and ornaments for her mother and sisters. She would encourage them: 'Ba, this looks good on you, and that on sister, spend some more and get it' or 'It does nothing for you'. She would express herself, share her views and take delight in seeing those she loved bedecked in finery. In her own case, while deciding the appropriateness

---

[4] *Abhijnana Shakuntala*, Act IV.

of clothing, she had formulated the principle outlined above. An ascetic consumes food as one consumes medicines; similarly, for Lilavati, finery was a way of protecting the family from social criticism. Lilavati neither sought nor accepted more.

48

Women aspire for bodily beauty just as they covet clothes and ornaments. Lilavati nurtured higher aspirations and kept desires in control, paid attention to non-physical aspects by subjugating bodily desires. In one of her notebooks, bare except for a verse, solitary like her, written on the centrefold:

Covering her head with her Sari,
Her face acquires a demureness of its own
She speaks a few words softly, intoning them sweetly,
She walks slowly, with her eyes downcast
O goddess mine: these are the
Marks of a pure and noble lineage.

The excerpted verse describes the moment when a Brahmin evaluates the character of the pious queen of Harsichandra as she was being sold as a servant in the streets of Kashi. The verse was used in *Sarasvatichandra* to describe the qualities of Saubhagya Devi.

The pure and high lineage of the queen was described by her clothes, face, speech, gait and gaze. Saubhagya Devi was also imagined to be noble and virtuous. The last line speaks of markers of lineage, pure and noble. Yet, many women of noble families are devoid of these. If we were to substitute 'pure and high penance' for 'pure and noble lineage', that would perfectly describe Lilavati. As I make this change in the stanza, Lilavati's image appears before me. Her sari, her demureness and her penance were like those described in the verse. She wrote the verse in the bare notebook, which shows her fondness for it as well as her own expectations from herself. Her life, one of illness and hardships, did not allow her to write the books that she could have; her notebooks remained bare, but just as a few stars light up a dark cloudy night, these scattered verses give a rare glimpse of her affective universe.

Why should the sari be worn in a particular way or the face display demureness, the gaze and gait be of a particular kind and her handwriting be such? Why were they what they were? They were so, not because of any physical desire or unrefined sentiment, but as a result of her most subtle aspirations. A student of music, devoted to the art of abstract sound, cultivates the muscles that produce sound, acquires mannerisms appropriate for the ability to produce such sound and these lend beauty to the performer. Similarly, Lilavati's body and mannerisms came to display her emotions through her speech, walk and gaze, rendering them beauteous.

The sense of belonging to a certain lineage does play a part but the lives of pious beings are enhanced by many other sources and we are able to grasp their emotions otherwise hidden and inarticulate, through their actions. Those who are capable of comprehending Lilavati's affective universe will be able to grasp the manifestations of that and those who do so will also understand the motivations and aspirations that guided her conduct, thus, getting a glimpse of the meaning of Lilavati's life.

49

The universe of a woman's desires is composed of bodily comforts, clothes, a circle of friends and the joy of participating in ceremonial functions. Lilavati's in-laws belonged to the town of Petlad. The town has many families of the Vadnagara Nagar caste and the women of these families are affectionate. They all had good things to say about Lilavati, and if they had a complaint, it was that she rarely stepped out of the house, did not visit anyone and had no friends; in short, she did not mingle and socialise with others. Those who saw this as a shortcoming, did not have any dislike for her, but they pitied her and made attempts to draw her out so that she did not become lonely and pitiable. She mingled and lived amicably with her in-laws and talked with them, she went to attend caste dinners or other ceremonies at such events and she spoke with all affectionately and heard them attentively. But she did ensure that such chatter did not exceed limits. Lilavati's elder brother-in-law had affection for this author even before Lilavati was born. She for this reason addressed him as Motibhai Kaka and his wife as Kapurba Kaki. Both of them took delight in Lilavati's happiness. After about a year of Lilavati's demise, her sister-in-law and her Kaka told this author tearfully, 'Lilavati did not have a single fault that could be pointed out. She was virtue personified.'

Though she was not at fault, this author once mentioned to her the criticism that she was subjected to. 'Moti, people say that you do not go out and mingle in Petlad at all, is this true? One should go out, meet a few people and converse with them.' She replied sombrely, 'Mota Kaka, what I do is right, and it is also proper that I stay by myself. Their way of life is not like ours. Their world is different.' The world around her played a different tune which was not pleasing to her and for that reason she preferred solitude. I, a curious ambler through the world of her emotions, did not expect a more elaborate answer. Satisfied with her response, I let her be.

If Lilavati ever sought anyone's company, it was that of her younger aunt—this author's younger sister—Samarthlaxmi. When Lilavati's father-in-law in his old age found employment in Junagadh, my sister was alive. She was enthused at the possibility that Lilavati would soon join her in that town as a resident. This aunt was very partial and attached to her niece. She could not even tolerate Lilavati's mother scolding her. She would draw Lilavati to her bosom and, exercising her right over the sister-in-law, she would say, 'Bhabhi! Ramnik is your only son. But I would always take Lilavati's side over him. If you were to ask me if I prefer Lilavati over Ramnik, my answer would be "yes". You are to say nothing to her.' This sister of mine, who encouraged me while I wrote Sarasvatichandra, left this world before Lilavati could join her in Junagadh. This author had to write an elegy for her in the third part of the novel. During the last phase of her illness, as she lay delirious, Lilavati sought the companionship of her aunt. 'Foi left before I could be with her in Junagadh, but now I am to go where she resides.' The niece expressed the need only for her company, such was the bond that they shared.

50

In this country and elsewhere, married women seek myriad pleasures. Men seek fulfilment through worldly pursuits or they expect fulfilment without the concomitant endeavour. Women, on the other hand, wish to elevate the life of daily grind in the household through festive celebrations, their lives are seen as fulfilled when they can find such pleasures. The joys of festivities are considered a pleasure. For several reasons, Lilavati would point to her one-year-old son and tell her mother-in-law, 'You should make him an ascetic!' Lilavati did not live long enough to see her son marry. She did not see her son's marriage as an occasion for great joy, but wanted a life of duty for her son. If she had lived to an age where her son had to be married, she would have probably surmised that 'My son is incapable of fulfilling his duties towards his wife.' This would have been a cause of concern for her. Lilavati believed that it was the duty of all mothers to train and equip their sons to fulfil their duties and advocated a life of celibacy for those who were incapable of this duty. She participated in the wedding celebrations of her younger sister with joy, but we have reasons to believe that she saw the occasion not only as one for pleasure but for support and hope. A woman intent on only pleasure does not think beyond here and now and the momentary, and for that reason they do not pause to consider if that son or daughter would find happiness in the times to come. On one hand, instead of becoming conscious of the duty towards the new daughter-in-law, they begin to cherish the expectations of the service that the daughter-in-law would carry out, on the other hand, instead of cultivating the daughter to acquire fitness to serve the mother-in-law, mothers hope that their daughters would be free from any such duty. Alongside festivities such aspirations also arise. Lilavati, however, did not observe her mother cherish such aspirations and we have seen how, instead, she was instructed by her mother to carry out her duties. Nurtured with such ideals, with a heart capable of reflection, she was indifferent to the transient pleasures of festivities. She hoped that her two sisters and her brother would find happiness in their respective marriages. She participated in the weddings of her sisters with these aspirations.

Before her death, she wanted her younger sisters to find happiness together with their husbands.

51

We will now be able to describe these worldly engagements of Lilavati who did not succumb to seeking pleasures but sought purposeful engagement with the world—a domain that is seen as belonging to the world of men. Most people are aware of their qualities but few know their faults. Poet Kalidasa has said that very few persons have the desire and the ability to see their faults and this quality is found among those who possess high and impartial intellect. Lilavati in her ever-so-short a life made a practice of finding her shortcomings and seeking to overcome them. Those who possess a sharp sense of auditory perception, their healthy ears can appreciate music and make an endeavour to sing. Those who possess clear, sharp, healthy eyes devoid of any disease can cultivate good handwriting and learn to draw well. In her childhood, Lilavati had smallpox and as a consequence for many years her eyes and ears were weak. As a child, she had a melodious voice but was unable to sing and her handwriting was not good. The author had instructed her teachers not to waste time over these so that she could be taught many other things in a short time, which the teachers accepted and followed. After several years of the early education, Lilavati became aware of her shortcomings and sought to remedy them. She got 'copy books' to improve her writing, but her illness prevented her from making beneficial use of them. She even attempted to improve her signing with the help of her younger sisters and cousins, but illness became an obstacle there too.

We have noted that in the course of her studies, she developed a certain dislike for English education and at that time she was allowed to have it her way and discontinue it. Since that day, she had not held an English book in her hands. At a stage when she thought of remedying her faults, she became conscious of her lack of knowledge in the English language. She had reached a stage when learning from a male teacher seemed inappropriate and, given the paucity of female teachers, she decided to learn the language through her own efforts. She found from the advertisement section of a Gujarati newspaper, a self-help book—*The Self-English Teacher.* She repeatedly urged this author to obtain the book through her uncle, the author's brother, Narhariram. Her illness became an obstacle in this effort as well. We have already discussed her attitude towards finery and clothing before her ailment, and especially how she adjusted to the condition of her in-laws while making choices. She always hesitated wearing fine clothes and ornaments, at the same time, she was also conscious of her own sense of inadequacy on this account. She tried to cultivate her feelings regarding this as well. She told her mother, 'Ba, sometimes, when I see Jasubehn decked up in fine clothes, I feel somewhat jealous, and until I can curb that feeling, I do not wish to wear good clothes, thus, training my mind to take delight in seeing Jasubehn in fine clothes.'

Everyone can understand the paucity of their material possessions. Intelligent persons know when they meet persons with superior intellect but rare are those self-aware persons who become conscious of undesirable feelings arising in them. The capacity to recognise one's own follies and to rid them from their roots and branches is a subtle art of those who have obtained mastery over their minds. Lilavati had acquired the skill to recognise her own faults and the necessary control over her mind to remedy them. All the sisters had equal possessions in terms of clothes and ornaments but the financial condition of their in-laws was different. Lilavati, devoid of wealth, was rich by her inner life and was hesitant to either accept or use objects such as clothes and ornaments. And yet momentary attachments impaired her subtle judgement, drawing her attention to her misfortune, vitiating her mind and at such times she would win over her feelings, establishing autonomy of her intellect and dispel the clouds. The shastras say that the wind that disperses clouds also brings together rain clouds, the mind that becomes desolate also has the capacity to garner fruits of the intellect. This has been said of those who have obtained mastery over their minds.

52

Why did Lilavati, who was otherwise capable of exercising control over her mind, feel that her lack of ability to sing or write in a good handwriting and her lack of knowledge of English were in fact her deficiencies?

Can it not be argued that she was enamoured of these aspects and the attraction clouded her judgement? Dear reader, having narrated so many aspects of Lilavati's life, my response to these posers is that she was neither attracted to singing nor ashamed of her handwriting and was not blinded by the shimmering glamour; and as I say this, I hope that you would have some faith in my words.

We have discussed in some details the practical use of Western knowledge for our women. Lilavati was cognisant of some of these aspects. Lilavati was taught at the very beginning of her education the statement from the *Niti Sataka*: 'A person, unacquainted with poetics, music and the arts, is, in fact, a beast without horns and tails.' As she grew in age, she became even more aware of the purpose of this saying. In the context of her life, the art of singing was quite well-developed among the women of Nagar community of Petlad. She found herself lacking in this art form and that was an obstacle in furthering her prestige in the community. Her mother also urged her to try and do better in that art, further her prestige and enhance the satisfaction of her husband. She also tried to improve her handwriting. Lilavati made sincere efforts to improve her signing and writing, satisfy her mother and attempt to give greater satisfaction to her husband and be true to her education. In fact, her younger aunt did not have these two shortcomings as her hand-writing was good and she sang melodiously. Lilavati found it beneficial to follow the example of her aunt. She was not unaware of the benefits of Western education either. Before she went to live at her in-laws', the book, written by the famous doctor of Junagadh, Tribhuvandas,[5] dealing with physiology and medicine, was placed in her hands. It is a difficult book to understand without the guidance of a teacher. But there are parts of the book that she could understand unaided, and it helped her till the very end. In her last days of illness, she was required to take various medicines at all hours of day

[5] Dr Tribhuvandas Motichand Shah (1850–1904), Assistant Surgeon and Chief Medical Officer, Junagadh State, pioneering plastic surgeon, wrote *Rhinoplasty* (1889) and *Maa Ne Shikhman*, the latter was used by M.K. Gandhi to help Kasturba give birth to their fourth son, Devadas Gandhi.

and night and follow a strict and disciplined regime. Her body weight was required to be measured and monitored, in those times patience and forbearance were as crucial as medication. In all this and all other matters of her illness and health, Lilavati could assist us and help herself. Her intelligence and reading from such books did play a significant role. She learnt the benefits of regular walks, of being in clean, fresh air—all this she had obtained from Western knowledge. During the early part of her illness, she could circumambulate the sacred tulsi plant and tried to get two benefits from one walk. She was taken to Mount Abu to help her recuperate. We had stayed in a bungalow on the Nakki Lake. She used to take walks on the promenade around the lake. She was advised to gradually increase her walk as her physical strength returned. She followed this advice. A person who was unable to walk more than a hundred feet walked three miles around the lake within a fortnight. Mount Abu is considered beneficial for the patients of tuberculosis, but those who know how to take the benefit tend to benefit more. She felt that her exposure to Western knowledge and modes of thinking had prepared her more for the sojourn, and for that reason, she sought to deepen her understanding of it. The Isa Upanishad celebrates a strong desire for life. This desire for life may or may not have been guiding her in the way envisaged by the Upanishad but she was filled with a will and a desire to live. Her Western learning had made not an insignificant contribution to her desire.

She was not content with receiving the education for herself. Before she died, she was told that the granddaughter of Bholanath Bhai[6]—Vidya[7]—had passed her BA examination. For a while, she forgot her pain and illness and exclaimed, 'Good, that is very good!' Her face glowed with joy. Her joy was similar to the joy of an ascetic at the wealth of a good and cultured person. I had begun her education with aspects of Western learning which were dropped in

[6] 'Rai Bahadur' Bholanath Sarabhai Divetia (1822–1886), a sub-judge in the colonial service, founded the Prarthana Samaj and Dharma Sabha in Gujarat.

[7] Lady Vidyagauri Neelkanth (1876–1958), daughter of Gopilal Dhruva and Balabehn, matriculated in 1891, graduated from Bombay University in 1901; she along with her sister Sharda Mehta were the first women graduates in Gujarat. Married Sir Ramanbhai Neelkanth.

accordance with her wish. But as she grew in age and experience, she sought that knowledge anew. What form it would have taken can only be speculated now as her search ended with her life.

53

The intermingling of Sanskrit learning and Western influences often manifested itself in delightful ways. During the period of her illness, as it is our custom, people would gather around her sickbed. There were times when she liked it, but other times, when she was ill-at-ease, even the sound of footsteps bothered her. Her mother would often sit in an adjacent room, keep an eye on her, incessantly pray and give out instructions for household chores. Sometimes, she would shout out instructions or a caretaker or a servant would enter her room noisily. Though Lilavati found this unbearable, she would say nothing and let things be.

One day, she told this author, 'What are we to do with our people? They do not understand what quietude is. How tranquil are the homes of the sahibs? And amongst us, illness implies hustle and bustle.' Her mother overheard this comment while she was trying to pray. She chimed in, 'What am I to do? I do not want your sleep disturbed, but there is one of me and tasks many, and I cannot manage it.' Lilavati laughed and said, 'Mota Kaka, I was not alluding to Ba only, but to our customs. In certain parts of Juangadh, there is a custom that as soon as a woman delivers a child, instead of giving her some quiet time, women gather around her bed and sing songs bereft of tune and melody.'

Even I could not help but laugh. 'Moti, such are the joys of auspicious occasions.'

'Mota Kaka, their joy is an assault on that poor woman. Our people do not have any understanding of tranquillity.'

By disposition, she sought peace and quiet, but when her health permitted, she would chat with those who had gathered around her bed. At times it seemed like she was delivering a discourse. If someone tried to stop her, she would retort, 'What is this notion of fairness wherein I am not to speak even when not in pain? What is to come, will, but in the last few days I told each one what they needed to be told.'

173

Once she had an occasion to speak to an Englishwoman. A gentleman named Pranlal Kahandas Joshipura was to travel to Bombay from Junagadh. Lilavati's elderly father-in-law decided to send her to Nadiad with this reliable companion. Lilavati was to travel in a third-class woman's compartment. Those were days of plague epidemic and third-class passengers had to undergo a lot of hardship of medical examination at the Wadhvan camp station. Therefore, Pranlal bought a first-class ticket for Lilavati and got her a seat in the first-class woman's compartment. Her fellow traveller was an Englishwoman who spoke Gujarati well. She and Lilavati talked about, among other things, customs of natives and Europeans. She told me of her encounter after she reached Nadiad. I asked her about their conversation, to which she replied, 'I told her bluntly, "Yes, our practice of child marriage is wrong, but equally wrong is your custom of widow remarriage."'

Lilavati! Vidyachatur, the man, is willing to sacrifice his ministerial position to get Kumud remarried, and that was a righteous decision! But Gunasundari, who had the forbearance of women, wanted something contrary to it, and that depiction is also appropriate to the delicacy of her character. You became a personification of that characterisation. There are differences among the leaders who espouse either old ideas or new. There are those thinkers who seek to secure the welfare of the country by a middle path and adopt ways suggested by you. They wish to abolish the practice of child marriage and wish to remain neutral with regard to the question of widow remarriage. They wish to remain neutral because opposition to widow remarriage is a violation of their duty and sense of justice and compassion. While, on the other hand, two other arguments are also valid—first, just as Dr Bhandarkar declared as the president of the Social Reform Association, that welfare of the country is not the same as the remarriage of some widows.

There are enough avenues for men and women for the expression of desire and passions. By adding to these opportunities, what we have hitherto considered civil in our social structure is likely to be under duress. This sense motivates even those whose hearts are just and compassionate.

This is not the place to examine this question from all its dimensions. Lilavati like some of these neutral thinkers believed that child marriage was a factor that contributed to the misery of our people. But among our common people these ideas appear fit only for the sahibs.

Lilavati from her sickbed engaged her mother and both her grandmothers in conversations about topics that interested them. On one such occasion, someone mocked and taunted her. 'Lilavati, I think you would like to be reborn as an Englishwoman.' As the general topic of conversation took this personal form, Lilavati was displeased. She was somewhat angry and retorted,

Why do you speak without a thought? I don't wish to be reborn either as an Englishwoman or as a Hindu. But if one is to be reborn, it cannot be said that to be born among us is superior to being born as a 'madam'. Our people following thousands of superstitions, make false claims and yet claim that we are moral and righteous. Aren't those who do not make false claims better? There is no end to the falsehood

176

among us, women steal from their husbands and mothers from their daughters. Similar conduct is seen among sisters. Is it not better to be born among the righteous and the virtuous among the sahibs than being born among us who promote falsehood? I do not wish to be reborn either among us or among them.

This exchange drained Lilavati. No one replied and the quietude that she liked prevailed.

6

Spiritual Awakening

54

We have hitherto glimpsed the social and worldly life of Lilavati, who desired no rebirth, be it happy or unhappy. We shall now try to look at her attempts to make sense of this world—which for her was unhappy and painful—to find repose and discern for herself modes of being in the world with equipoise. She had captured the essence of life through three words—*dukkha* (pain/sorrow); *chitta* (consciousness) and *jivan* (life). We shall construe these three categories.

55

When we came to know of Lilavati's illness and called her to Nadiad from Junagadh, she wrote in a letter dated 2 January 1901:

Shirchhatra[1] Pitaji,

I have your letter.[2] I am appraised of the news you gave. My body remains indifferent, if it is well for two days, it is weak for the following two. I take medications prescribed by a doctor. I cannot say when I would be able to come to Nadiad, because I would have to travel with everyone else and would have to wait till the time means are found for all of us to travel. Most probably it will be after Holi.

Your letter gives me solace. I know that *dukkha*, *chitta* and *jivan*—all three are transient. And yet, some days, it gives me agony and I try and divert my mind by telling that whatever the

---

[1] In Gopalkrishna Gandhi's rendering; 'ennobled and ennobling canopy of protection'.

[2] This letter and the letter that G.M.T. wrote in response to this are at Appendices 1 and 2.

God does—either good or bad—is ultimately for
our own good. And I have read:

'Even the moon, the one who plays about in the
firmament,
Destroys all darkness, wields a thousand rays,
And is at the centre of all planets and astral
bodies,
Because of destiny even he is
Swallowed, during eclipse by Rahu,
Who can erase what is predestined?'[3]

When even the moon faces erasure and pain,
who are we? Moreover, it is said:

'God bestows joys and miseries like a mother
Giving pills and potions bitter and sweet
These miseries are veiled blessings from God
The surgeon who makes an incision on the body,
Has a heart no less kinder than our lord's?'[4]

---

[3] Translated from the original Sanskrit for this work by Arindam
Chakraborty.
[4] Translated from the original Gujarati for this work by Prathistha
Pandya.

And I am convinced that whatever God does, is for our welfare. Kindly do not worry about me. Give me the news of your bodily health. Do write about the fever that mother had. I am worried about her. Do tell me if I can do anything for you. Please forgive me for my errors and omissions, my blessing to Chi. Bhai[5] and others.

Pranam,
Lilavati.

These were the thoughts on *dukkha* that she had expressed in her letter. She used to say that in times of suffering one should look at those whose suffering is even greater. She would often repeat the shastra, which said 'Mind alone is the cause of bondage and freedom',[6] to remove from the root the poison of sorrow. The agony one has to suffer was to be borne without blaming God for it; it has to be seen as beneficial and accepted as a potion of nectar.

---

[5] 'Chi.' is short of 'Chiranjeevi', meaning one with long life.
[6] Verse 2 of the *Brahmabindu* Upanishad.

56

These are the ways in which she tried to understand pain, suffering, *dukkha*. The cause of suffering, of bondage, is in the mind alone. It would be an unnecessary repetition to say that she tried to free her mind. This life story is a narration of her mind, it is a depiction of the pictures that her mind presented. She considered destiny and God's will to be the same and with that faith dealt with her pain. Her mind was not feeble and did not experience either the helplessness or meekness akin to a cow caught in a quagmire. Her desire for life was not devoid of purpose and endeavour. The aspirations of women are often contained by their households, which was not the case with Lilavati. She had a sense of higher purpose about the fact of her life. This was to make her life fruitful. dukkha, *chitta* and *jivan* may have been fleeting and transient, but she addressed them through her 'notebook'.

Get up, get up, get up early, get up you, oh
woman!
You are brave, and of noble birth why lie and
die in misery?

You are bewildered I see, and blinded by terror.
    But would you hide to escape the horror?
    You passionately observe your vows, that
        passion is misplaced
Destiny is irreversible, don't mourn oh woman!
    The doors are all shut, would you die of
        exasperation?
Come cross the courageous threshold, walk into
        the open field
Life is too short, come act, you must play
        your part
Noble blood, noble death, are subjects of
        happy song.[7]

She, the one experiencing the agony of life, knows that her life is short, she is aware that she must play her assigned part and yet, as these lines suggest, she must give up her bewilderment and fear and step across the courageous threshold and walk into the open field. Lilavati gave up the meekness of a cow and like a lioness crushed attachment and mourning

---

[7] Translated from the original Gujarati for this work by Prathistha Pandya.

under her paws. What did she wish to achieve through this endeavour? Unlike the lioness, she was not moved by an impulse to assuage her hunger but wished the welfare of others. What means did she have for such selfless and unattached action?

The *Niti Shataka* that she had studied says, 'Everyone, though overtaken by difficulty, desires a fruit according to their inborn disposition.'[8] The fruits that Lilavati desired in her time of agony was according to her disposition. It is said with respect to those who feel the pain of others that God created the sun, the moon, rains, trees, rivers and cows and righteous persons for the welfare of others. This life story has illustrated that Lilavati, ever righteous, even when meek and in bondage like a cow, always sought to do good for others. She did not harbour any desire for gratification and God created her not for the enjoyment of the world but for the welfare of others. Her efforts and endeavours were determined by her in-born disposition, and that effort flows through my heart in the form of the song given above.

---

[8] Verse 30 of the *Niti Shataka*.

She had studied the Gita with the capacity she had, which describes unsullied faith as natural to noble persons. Such unsullied faith, like a bottomless well, nourished her mind and its sweet waters satiated all those who drank from the well that was her life. The hearts of great souls are aglow with righteousness; its source perennial and pure manifests through their actions. The judgement about Lilavati's life must not be done by her proud father but by good, cultivated and impartial readers. But this author does consider it within the rubric of his capacity to characterise Lilavati's quest as spiritual and not gross.

57

What is considered sorrow by others, Lilavati viewed that as a means of welfare. We have also seen how she shunned pleasure and self-gratification. Our experience suggests that average human beings tend to remain unenlightened and are weighed down by both sorrow and joy. They seek to embrace joy and are crushed by the sorrow that befalls them. Both these are signs of unenlightened beings. It is said, 'With each passing day, an unenlightened person becomes ever more sinful, cruel and pitiable', while enlightened souls like Janaka say, 'If the mind becomes attached to worldly riches, it begets desire and effort, I consider these as great calamities.' Other great souls have said that riches are the source of troubles, and wealth opens doors to calamities which rush in through them. If one does not regard the lure of riches as undesirable, it directs human endeavours in that direction. Any endeavour that seeks the lure of wealth alone is undesirable for some, the onset of difficulties propels the courageous towards action—action that benefits others as well. In moments of immense pain and agony, Lilavati remained intent upon God and hoped that agony would in God's hands be transformed into the most supreme of outcomes. It is appropriate to consider that the moment this faith and aspiration combined in her, she opened up the path of welfare for herself. Society makes endeavours to secure riches regardless of the means of their attainment. She considered it a violation of morality to seek riches—however limited—from her father's home. She was also aware that other avenues of obtaining wealth were closed for her. Lilavati remained free from desire and considered calamites that came her way as a path to upliftment. Many human beings are unable to free themselves from the agonies of desire even while seeking a glimpse of truth.

Do not carnal desires appear gross? They do. Why do humans hunger for them? The reason is that desire is life itself. It does not leave us. The body withers till death comes. The heart knows that one should covet only Brahma, truth. And yet, what is the nature of desire that despite being contrary to reason, deepens and torments to the good in us?

Divine grace kept Lilavati free from the agony that even the righteous have to endure. There are those who describe carnal desire as debased, body as subject to decay and life as transient. They characterise siblings as coming together of wayfarers who are destined to separate and hence ultimately cause pain. They describe worldly pursuits as futile and meaningless and, for that reason, it's something to be shunned, they proclaim such things but very few are able to abide by the truth of it.

The hearts of the pious are thus imbued with a spirit of renunciation, some of them forsake all outward attachments while others accept the situation they find themselves in. They desire neither renunciation nor worldly attachments; they accept God's will and do their duty while remaining unattached to the fruits of their actions. This second path is also a path of renunciation as shown by Janaka. The reader who has been attentive to the propositions of this life story need not be told that Lilavati followed this path of renunciation both at her in-laws' and at her natal home.

58

A mind that's uplifted experiences quietude but that is not the end of their upward rise. Just as the blooming of flower results in coming of the fruit, a heart that's tranquil begins to experience the emergence of philosophical disposition. Philosophical disposition remains unmanifested. How is it to be captured by speech? If the essence of the world view eludes speech, is it futile to argue that a student receives the knowledge through the mere presence of a benevolent teacher? There are those who are learned because of a teacher or through some other means. There are those whose only disposition is that of compassion towards all beings and, though learned, they know that they are ignorant and the means of attaining knowledge from the state of ignorance are known to them. They are imbued with this faith and their hearts know what the intellect cannot make intelligible. Adept men remove all obstacles that come in the way of knowledge; and, as it was said earlier, the blooming flowers bring fruits with them. Goodness once attained does not vanish with the body. The Gita says that one who does good is never overcome by evil.[9]

The Indic civilisation has since very ancient times believed that goodness once attained ensures a heart free of evil, and such a heart experiences with renewed vigour a sense of fulfilment, the presence of God and righteous disposition. We shall conclude this life story after acquainting ourselves with these aspects of Lilavati's heart.

---

[9] Discourse 6, verse 40.

59

A question is usually posed about the fulfilment of the lived life for those who consider the worldly life as futile and illusory like a dream world. Some accuse the seekers of salvation that their quest is solitary and self-serving.

When Sage Vasistha sought the answer to the mystery of a long life—life as long as eons—from Sage Bhushundi, he counselled:

I neither praise, nor censure anyone; nor anything at anytime; my mind does not exult on gaining what is considered good; nor does it become depressed on obtaining what is considered evil; hence my state of happiness and health. I embrace the supreme renunciation, having renounced even the desire to live; thus, my mind does not entertain cravings, but is peaceful and balanced.[10]

[10] *Yoga Vasistha*, translated by Swami Venkatesananda (Delhi: Motilal Banarasidas, 2003), p. 246.

Lord Vishnu advised Prahlad about his duties as he neglected his kingdom in his immersion in Vishnu:

> You are free from attachment and detachment, how can cravings have any impact on you? Hence, awake and rise. You, a *Jivan Mukta*, have to perform your duties till the end of time. Death befits only those whose intellect is trapped by fears such as, "I am weak, I am in agony." Death befits only those who are ensnared by desires and whose mind is unsteady. One who is devoid of pride, whose intellect is uncompromised, who is equable to all beings has a life of glory. One devoid of attachment and hatred observes all as a witness does, his heart calm and his life glorious.

A *Jivan Mukta*—one who is freed from life and rebirth—does not consider life as something to be renounced and death as worthy of embrace. Such a person does not consider life of a householder as one that needs to be shunned and life of a forest dweller as the one which is to be adopted. Because for a *Jivan Mukta*, life and death, household and forest are not categories of contemplation. It is the duty

Spiritual Awakening

of such a person to keep the body alive till it meets the end. Similarly, whatever the illusory, dreamlike world offers, the *Jivan Mukta* accepts and seeks neither to improve it nor shun it as undesirable. Such a person does not ponder over sorrow and regard life as painful. They do not seek to withdraw from the currents of life and they regard life and its vicissitude as work of God and thus remain without the ego of the one who acts. They consider it their duty to deal with all those who come into their contact with a sense of equanimity and make the endeavours necessary for sustenance of the body.

The counsel to Prahlad also instructs us the duties of human life, and the fulfilment that has to be sought in that endeavour. All objects and beings that come before the liberated one are regarded with the same equable gaze and with an awareness that they too are imbued with God. The supremacy of God is thus evident. And such a person submits to the omnipotence of God and worships that power lovingly and takes delight in its manifestation and in worshipful service. Self-realisation is the realisation of the divine. A liberated person purifies the mind by delving deep within that realisation.

It remains untouched and unsullied by ego and other corruptions. The qualities enumerated by Sage Bhushunga—forbearance in times of trouble, equability in times of riches, the delicacy of heart that partakes of joys and sorrows of others and the capacity for friendship—are the qualities of the liberated one. Therein lies virtue, purity, realisation of God, bliss and meditative oneness with God. The being that finds elevation thus attains fulfilment.

60

As described in section 4 of this life story, Lilavati maintained *Vajra*-like hardness in times of agony, she embraced pain like how Mirabai drank poison, as if it were nectar. The same section describes how she cultivated a sense of friendship with the world, the prayer that she did not offer for herself was the prayer that she offered to seek healing for the world from plague and famine. All that she could do to ameliorate the suffering of the world was to offer prayers, which she did. She dealt with all persons, be they at her natal home or the house of her in-laws, with poise and generous affection, she was noble towards them and happy in their joy and unhappy in their suffering. She made tremendous effort to reduce her pain and enhance their joy. Her life story is suffused with such examples. Her endeavour was without any self-interest, she, in fact, sacrificed herself in the attempt. She regarded the world as futile but played her part in the drama of life, she remained indifferent to her pain, the suffering that came as the will of God. She remained firm in her resolve that she would not let tears moisten her eyes. She remained unperturbed in pain and equable in joy; dealt with both conditions with sweetness, gentleness and goodness. Her life is a commentary on life's stages of pain, consciousness and being.

61

Now we shall see the nature of the divine, of the God that Lilavati held in her heart. There are many dispositions on the nature of the divine prevalent in the world: some are non-believers, some have faith in idol worship, some believe that God and all other beings are distinct, while others believe in the non-duality of God and beings. There were persons of all these types around Lilavati. Her maternal grandmother Laherlaxmi worshipped all gods—Hindu and Muslim alike. She had more faith in divine grace than medicines, she belonged to the Swaminarayan sect, was deeply devout and keen to do good to others. She always taught her daughter to serve the mother-in-law, to have greater regard for the mother-in-law in comparison to the mother. Lilavati often entered into a discussion with her so that she could learn from her faith and qualities. Lilavati's paternal grandmother, that is this author's mother, Shivakashi, had detached herself from these worldly entanglements around the same time when this author also sought to detach himself from these worldly affairs on day-to-day basis. Shivakashi spent her days in prayer and worship. A temple was built in the memory of this author's father to fulfil his wish and Shivakashi spent her days in worshipping her chosen god, Shrinathji, at this temple. She tended to remain detached from both auspicious and inauspicious occasions and sought fulfilment in prayer. She had renounced outward entanglements and sought to free herself from the desires of her heart. But her mind was often an obstacle in this effort. Lilavati would often tell her, 'Moti Ba, your prayers and worship would bear fruit when your mind is purified and you are able to cultivate a disposition that is described in the story of exemplars. If you think that you can gain fruits through the elaborate worship, you are mistaken.'

Lilavati's paternal grandfather, this author's father, was a devout Vaishnava. He was not a follower of any Goswami Maharaj. But he worshipped the *Shaligram* with the fulfilment of rituals, he had offered his heart to God and considered all that life offered him as divine gift; he studied the Gita and other texts and sought out sections that deal with the relationship between God and humans and devotion of the latter. He spent a large part of the day and night in heartfelt worship, prayer, reading religious texts and listening to katha and other religious observances. In the first half of his life, he was a moneylender in Bombay, and even then, he spent his days as described above. Whosoever experienced the simplicity of his heart believed him to be a man of ascetic disposition. Some even considered him to be like Narsinh Mehta. He had deep faith in rituals. When he heard the Sama Veda being recited by a priest or when he recited it himself, his heart would mingle with its tune and cadence. Lilavati, while growing up and even later, had seen her grandfather as worshipful, devout, detached and pure. And these righteous aspects had made an impression on her heart early on. This author has reasons to believe that when Lilavati pointed out to her grandmother the error of her ways, she had the example of her grandfather before her and she was guided by it.

Merely seven or eight days before her body eventually gave up, Lilavati's illness suddenly took a turn for the worse, early one morning. This author took her words as a form of hysteria and sought to remedy that. Lilavati knew that the remedy proposed was futile and regaining equanimity at the time of crisis, she said, 'Mota Kaka, what are you waiting for? This is not hysteria, give me medication, I need warmth, my hands and feet have turned cold and yet I am sweating.' She was right. If her instructions were not adhered to, she would have died that very instant and we would not have had the benefit of her presence and companionship for the additional seven–eight days. Even at the moment when death seemed imminent, at a moment of fear, she gave the instructions and then drew her attention to other matters. It seemed that her life was about to leave her body in a minute or even half, and at that time she had the presence of mind to give instructions and then she focused on chanting the name of God. Even that chant was done intelligently and with awareness. 'Oh, superstitious *Parameshwar* of Laheriba! Oh, *Prabhu* of Dadaji! Oh, *Paramatma* of Mota Kaka!' She addressed the divine in different ways and repeated the names. She was saved by God. At such moments, many repeat the name of Rama, but those reciting the name rarely pause to ask if the person for whose benefit the recitation is taking place can hear the name or if the recitation is meaningful to the dying person. Sometimes, the lack of meaning in recitation is due to the condition of the body, sometimes it is the lack of cultivation of the heart and, when such cultivation is not entirely absent, its lessons may not have cast deep roots in his heart. This incident is illustrative of the cultivation of Lilavati's heart.

Fanatic and sectarian persons are unable to see God in any other form than the one which has been enshrined in their hearts; they consider forms that are enthroned in the hearts of others as deviant and criticise not only that form but the belief that lies at the root of it. A liberal intellect is able to see one form in the myriad images and in their mind's eye the divine attains an unsullied and complete form. Lilavati, moved by such liberal spirit, had sought the pure form of God while she was in good health which became apparent in the moment of crisis. Lilavati had seen invocation of God in many forms and ways since childhood. Her illiterate but good-natured grandmother invoked God in one way, her devout grandfather experienced God in his heart in a different way, while her father intellectually understood God in another way. She could see that while her invocation was different, the essence was the same. She had seen, even among her close family, a difference of attitudes of devotion and forms of worship. She had studied texts that had taught her the distinction between spirit and the matter. She had read the Isa and Ken Upanishads and the Gita at a young age and she had grappled with, in the context of her age and comprehension, various forms of the divine. During the course of her life she had pondered over these without the guidance of a teacher and eventually all that churning manifested itself in the essence of her heart. She could see that her grandmother, her grandfather and her father, according to their disposition and capability, eventually worshipped one divine form, and her utterance captured both their difference and unity.

62

Now the only aspect that we need to narrate is how these high aspirations of fulfilment of life and the desire to realise God manifested itself in Lilavati's life, especially in terms of its ability to temperance of instincts.

A spiritual life makes instincts less powerful and once they have been subjugated, the passions of the sense organs also subside; only their traces remain and they are replaced by a tranquil force which is the joy of peace. This bliss remains even when the body is in pain or experiences pleasure, when the mind is fearful and weeps. When the cruel emperor Nero punished the philosopher Seneca by cutting open his veins, though in excruciating pain and writhing in agony, that great soul gave a philosophical discourse to his loved ones seated by his side and gave up his life thus discoursing. Just as laughing loudly is not always an expression of pure joy, crying out in agony is an instinctive response that does not preclude joy. And for that reason, pure joy is considered perennial and is also described as a state of joylessness. It is said, 'There is joy in tears as well.'[11] This was said of the peculiar nature of happiness. When the body in pain makes one cry in agony, the consciousness is capable of bearing witness to this pain and the same consciousness is also capable of experiencing joy at the time when the body is in pain. It is akin to an adult laughing when the child weeps. A person bears witness to his own death in a dream and in rare moments that dreaming mind also becomes aware of its dreamlike state and the fact that eventually the dream would be over. Bliss, that which is eternal, arises with the awareness of the true nature of the divine and imbues human life with new piety. This bliss is a result of the spiritual growth previously described.

---

[11] This statement is in Hindi in the original.

As Lilavati matured in age and ideas, she did experience such bliss to some extent. As described in section 53, as soon as she was relieved of the bodily pain, she would put that immediate experience behind her and engage enthusiastically in conversation around her. Her capacity for joy, bottled up by physical ailment, would spring forth like a fountain whose valve had been turned on.

Her doctor had advised that her bodily weight be measured every seven days to monitor the progress of her tuberculosis. Each measurement brought a lower figure, bringing the footsteps of Yamaraj closer each passing day. The group that weighed her assumed that progressive reduction would cause her pain and for that reason averted her eyes or obfuscated the reading. The attempt was futile. The more they tried to cheat her, the more alert she became, she even joked, 'All of you apprehend that I would be shocked to know the truth! Your assumption has been wrong on both the counts. I know the truth and I am not shocked by it.' She had read books on the nature of the disease. Everyone around her was pained that their association with her was not going to last long but this short-lived association was not the source of pain for Lilavati. A child is excited at the prospect of travel to a new place, is enthused by the possibility of travel by train and the prospect of seeing new scenes and meeting different people and usually would spend the days preceding the travel joyously. Lilavati's joy, though not childish, was similar and she spent her remaining days in the company of people who gave her joy. A person, uninvolved, watches water pour out of a vessel with holes, similarly, she watched life ebb out of her body with equanimity. She was neither unhappy nor fearful. This author remembers her mental condition as akin to a viewer in a bemused state, waiting for a new act of a play to unfold. She could retain her poise even in pain; albeit severe agony did cloud her face at times. She could partake of joy when pain receded, but would not allow joy to be unbridled. We shall bring this narration to a close after looking at one such example.

63

Once Lilavati had come to Nadiad to participate in some function. At that time, she was healthy and seemed happy to be with her parents and siblings. One day, around 5 p.m., the band played outside our house to mark the wedding celebrations in the family of a relative. The groom's party was about to set out in the wedding procession. Lilavati's mother, her brother, sisters and servants of the family all went out to participate in the festivities and witness the beginning of the procession. There was no one left in the house. The last person to step out shouted, 'Bhai, watch the door!' I was reading and writing in my room on the first floor. I went to the window and inquired, 'Who is in the house?' 'Lilavati behn is the only one', came the reply. When everyone had gone out to participate in the festivities, why was Lilavati the only one to be left behind? This bothered me. My house is unusually long and the distance between the front and the backyard is more than other houses. If I were to call out from the upstairs front room, Lilavati who was in the rear would not have heard me. I wanted to know why she had chosen to stay away from celebrations, but I was more curious to know what she was doing with herself. I quietly walked from my room to the terrace on the back and peered down. I found

Lilavati seated with her back resting against a wall. Her visage was tranquil and somber. She softly sang a verse, again and again. She recited it to a rhythm, the beat of which she gave with her right hand on her right thigh. What was that verse?

Curbing the desire, practising patience, giving
    up pride, not interested in committing a sin,
Speaking the truth, following the footsteps of
    the good, serving the scholars,
Respecting the honourable, pleasing even
    enemies, being modest,
Protecting fame and being kind towards the
    distressed. These are the actions of the good.

My footsteps did thud in the terrace but Lilavati was so engrossed in herself that did not hear it. She did not look up. I did not wish to break her rhythm or disturb the picture of pious beauty that she presented. She recited the verse with her mind absorbed in the meaning of the words. Not only her mind but her body too seemed to respond to the deeper meaning of the verse. As she said 'slay the desires', her raised hand came down forcefully, when she said 'forgiveness', her forefinger also signalled forgiveness, the injunctions of the verse were enacted by her hand and they came to be etched in her mind and with that, both the hand and the mind seemed tranquil, this meditative moment filled her mind with contentment which spread on her face. I retreated without disturbing that picture, that meditative moment and satisfaction that it accorded to her. The festivities that ordinary women and men had commenced gave no bliss to her heart; she found her solitary joy and remained immersed in it.

The author could get a glimpse the fruits of her lifelong endeavour in this expression of unsullied joy. Even when pain cast a shadow over her, the joy she experienced was the same joy. On that day, the unblemished joy that freely expressed itself through her was the result of the meditative state that she had attained in accordance with her capacity. The verse upon which she meditated intently contained the guidelines, the injunctions for the life that she wanted. Adherence to these norms made it possible for the Great Will to manifest itself in her heart; her unadulterated joy bore testimony to that presence. Her proud father has considered that fulfilment, that grace of the divine as the attainment of non-duality by her. She had not become learned through the study of many books; she was part of no adventure, she received no bodily pleasure, nor did she seek it; but the manifestation of her inner life, whose light was as soothing as the sun at dawn, gave her meaning and made her life auspicious.

64

Lilavati! You are now un-manifest. But for all those doing penance like you did, and those who have, like you, attained a measure of spiritual attainment, my heart repeats your name, and through that utterance seeks:

I feel as if this earth is blooming with flowers and pleasant leaves with the stepping of both your radiant feet. May trees be laden with the flowers, weighing heavier than tender leaves and flowers, sprouting/sprouted fearlessly since birth.[12]

---

[12] Translated from the original Sanskrit for this book by Jyotirmaya Sharma.

It is also possible that there may be a reader, compassionate of heart, Westernised and yet imbued with the spirit of this land. To that reader I would say in a language more familiar: 'Dear friend! This is the land of the Aryas, see the meaning of this life story through that.'

> Stranger! This is India! Here her daughter's laid!
> Such was her law, and she that law obey'd!

Appendices

Appendices

Appendix 1

The Author's letter to Lilavati

Nadiad, Friday
Maha Vad 11, Samvat 1957

Chi. and Akhand Saubhagyavati Lilavati[1]

Both your mother and I have written several letters but there is not one from you. There has been no letter for at least a month and that worries me. Reply to me as soon as you receive this letter and therein write in

---

[1] *Akhand Subhagyavati* means 'eternally fortunate'.

detail and truthfully about your bodily wellbeing and about Chi. Bhana.[2] If I do not receive a letter from you within the next eight to ten days, I would send Icchashanker or someone else to Junagadh to bring you here. Therefore, reply by the return post. If you did not write due to laziness or some such thing, do not be lazy about this henceforth. And if you are unable to write due to bodily ailment get someone in the house to write or get Harsukhram to write for you.

I remain, of late, rather worried about your bodily health and other matters of your life. It has been four long months, all of you have been ill and yet obstinately remain there. I have not been able to provide means other than the education given to you for securing your welfare in such times. That education and your forbearance should not forsake you at such times. Now all that is given me to do is to provide counsel through letters from time to time. I have chosen to retire but in that I take this new responsibility. I hope that God will grant me success in this endeavour. You understand all things, your welfare lies in remaining peaceful.

---

[2] Lilavati's infant son, G.M.T.'s grandson.

God gives sorrow to human beings. When such sorrow falls to the lot of evil-minded people, it is considered to be a punishment for their sins. But when God gives pain to someone like you, whose life is unblemished, it is to be deciphered as the karma of previous lives, as one receives the fruits of the good deeds of the present life in the lives to come. It is for this reason that they say— neither happiness nor sorrow are perennial, like the wheels of a cart, what is below comes up and what is ascendant comes down, so life comprises joy and suffering. Once there was affluence in the family of your father-in-law, which turned to pecuniary hardship and the wheels of fortune have not turned so far, and you found your share in this unhappiness. When good times return, you will get a share in that too, with this faith you should not lose your patience. God will look after you. I am a mere man but your care is not lost to the God. He would do good by you, have that faith and earn his blessing and all will be well. I lack the ability to ameliorate your suffering in this life. But God has the power to take away all pain and suffering from all the births destined for you. For this reason, one need not pay attention to a person's goodwill or lack thereof, or to their words. Do your duty such that God grants you peace and happiness in all the lives to come. When Jayanti got cholera, we got her to focus her mind on the goddess and on Mahadev. You live in a distant land, no one here knows your true condition. But if your body is well enough to allow you to read and benefit from this letter, do so; your education has made you capable of that. You do not write and no one writes to us about your condition and that I consider our fate. But I know that the God who granted you education and virtue will also give you joy and suffering, pass you through ordeals and offer you a soothing shade and eventually bring fruition to your life. Keep your mind happy and have faith in God and do not give up the hope of receiving his grace. Those who retain faith in God are never forsaken by him. I will wait for your letter for eight to ten days, failing which I will send someone to Junagadh to bring you here.

Well wisher
Govardhanram's blessings

Appendix II

The Author's letter to Lilavati

Nadiad
March 10, 1901
Chi. and Akhand Saubhagyavati Lilavati,

You would have been in receipt of the letter that I dictated and had sent to you. When we know that your body and mind are happy, we regain our equanimity and when we receive no letters from you, we worry. Even if you cannot write a detailed letter, you could write on a card 'I am well' or 'I have fever'. Yesterday, I wrote to Dr Chhaganlal of Junagadh and to Murabbi Manibhai Kaka that you should be sent, if the doctor so advises, to Nadiad with an attendant otherwise you should be treated there. You should follow the advice of the doctor. The proposed journey of your family has been delayed but you need not wait for all of them to travel with you to Nadiad. You should not go against the doctor's advice.

In your previous letter, you cited a verse and said words to assuage my concerns that has given me peace of mind. In England, young girls determine their own destiny but in our country the parents decide the fates of their daughters. The generosity and piety of our daughters for that reason is superior. Those daughters who are content to seek the welfare of the in-laws and are satisfied with their fate perform an act of charity on their parents, because it is the parents who have given such circumstances to their daughters in their new homes. The supreme father of all the parents, God, at times, sets aside suffering for us and that too must be accepted as one accepts bitter medication—you understand this well and seek solace in that understanding. One should consider it immeasurable grace of God that he gave you the intellect to comprehend this. Great souls among us have said that we should consider riches to be transient because they grant no happiness. It is the norm of the world that the rich fears even their own sons.

It is also said that nothing that we see in the world is permanent. Persons accumulate wealth on the strength of their good deeds but the same wealth turns into a source of misery as it becomes a passion by itself.

There is great wisdom in these two perspectives. I know that you would comprehend it if I were to elaborate their meaning.

Many among us lead a religious life to either propitiate God or to earn merit or wealth from such observances. Desire is a form of greed. And religious observances done with expectations of its fruits is action based on desires. Those who follow religion to either save themselves from pain or in the desire to obtain happiness do likewise and when their wishes are granted it is seen as a boon from God. What this society considers as happiness has been considered passions in our shastras. Kingship and ministerial positions are passions and so is wealth. Those who perform meritorious acts or observe religion in desire of such passions cease to do them once their passions are fulfilled and at such time the passions begin to act according to their nature. A person obtains great wealth as a result of a great endeavour and after much hardship. But what reward does wealth bring? There is conflict and strife in the family of a wealthy person, there are disputes among their children to gain a greater share of the wealth. This produces attachments, ego, pride and jealousy. Sometimes, the wealthy wish to spend their money in the wrong way, they splurge and became devoid of virtue. Therefore, the ultimate outcome of religious observance done for desires is undesirable.

Therefore, one should expect no fruits of our action and those observances done without any expectation of its fruits is called desireless action and such worship is an act of faith in the divine. A person so devoted considers sorrows as a bitter medicinal potion sent by God and continues to follow the righteous path. This forbearance in face of suffering is a kind of yoga. And those who attain this state are yogis and their suffering is a form of penance. A person who follows religion in hope of fruits thereof eventually finds sorrow while a desireless devotee turns suffering into a source of strength such that unhappiness has no effect on him. Those who become yogis eventually become *Jivan Mukta*. Others might obtain heaven after death but such a person obtains peace and deliverance in this life. There is a saying, 'Knowledge that cannot grant peace is no knowledge'. Not all learned men understand this but you thought that one should view suffering as a bitter medicinal potion. This is a rare outcome of learning. When the seeds of such knowledge are sowed deep and well, they invariably grow into fruit-bearing trees. God has sown the seed of wisdom, nurture it with rectitude and the ultimate fruit and joy will emerge from your present sorrow. You must remember your study of the Gita—a being passes through many lives and ripens like grains through the suffering that it endures and eventually attains the state of deliverance, of ultimate freedom. The happiness obtained from religious observances done in expectation of fruits thereof tend to be transient while the bliss of desireless action is perennial.

I too had to face many hardships when I was your age but I too considered it as a bitter medicine sent by God and today I reap its benefits. At that age, I had written a verse which said that a considerate and intelligent father pushes his son in the ocean of suffering so that he may achieve happiness in the future; similarly, the all-seeing father gives unbearable sorrow to his progeny to give them the ultimate boon.

I am happy that you are having similar thoughts that I had at your age. Have faith that God will do well just as he did in my case and, believing so, do your duty. The third wife of Shastri Jivaram died in Bombay from fever.

Well wisher
Govardhanram's blessings

Appendix III

Letter from Ganpatram Anupram Tarvadi

Surat
Near Burhanpuri Bhagol
Pagathia Sheri
2 February 1902, Sunday, 3 p.m.

Learned Govardhanramji,

It was only a short time ago that I learnt that all the medications and other remedies that you employed failed and Behn Lilavati now resides in the heaven!

I lived in Junagadh for two and a half years. I was the next-door neighbour of Ra. Ra. Manilal Bhai and for that reason I was acquainted with the education that she had received, her noble virtues and other qualities that our women should emulate. They were a source of pleasant surprise for me. My wife also took solace in the reincarnation of her dear and departed friend, Samarthlaxmi, in her.

It is natural that you would deeply mourn the passing of such a daughter. But as I addressed you in the beginning of the letter, I consider you 'learned'. And for that reason, instead of daring to give you solace, both of us express the purest sentiments and goodwill of our hearts for your family.

Ganpatram Anupram Travadi's Namaskar

Appendix IV

An Elegy Written and Presented by the
Nadiad Nagar Youth Committee[3]

The world mourns the death of Lilavati,
Who went to heaven at the age of twenty
Lilavati, Lilavati, the ideal daughter of mine
English and Sanskrit she knew, spoke in her mother
    tongue with ease
A virgin kind and content, with noble virtues that please
Faithful to her husband, a maiden virtuous and pure
Like Kusum in *Sarsvatichandra*, the father is blessed
He performs the pious duty, educates his daughter well
Bound by duty without self-aggrandise, blessed is
    Govardhanram
Not many fathers like him exist in the village of
    Nadiad
Let God's will prevail, our efforts are of no avail
The one who is missed on this earth was missed in
    heaven as well

---

[3] Translated from the original Gujarati for this work by Prathistha
Pandya.

Death is the final truth we know, and that is no
    cause for sorrow
It's the flaw in our fate that we leave things
    unfinished and imperfect
We pray to our Lord every day for the wellbeing of
    our women
Wishing them the love of their loved ones and peace
    when in heaven.

Appendix V

Letter from Chhaganlal Harilal Pandya to the Author[4]

Junagadh
6 January 1902

My dear Govardhanbhai,

I have been watching with great anxiety the progress
towards the recovery of our Lilavati Ben, and the
accounts received some days ago being hopeful, I

---

[4] The original letter is in English.

was under the impression that she would regain her health in the course of time. But I learn today from my mother that she has again had a relapse and that the condition of the poor dear girl is critical.

I can well imagine how you, who are on the spot, feel to see a dear pet child—reared with as much care and attention—fast sinking in spite of all the medical aid a fond father's love could bring to bear on the case. Verily, the privations . . .[5]and the exertions she had to make in order to keep the family wheel going are the bottom of the evil . . .[6]All we could do was to sympathise with her and lessen her burden as far as practicable. You have spared no pains to keep her contended and happy, but her physical constitution has proved too weak to resist the attacks of fever brought on by a sensitive mind and work without rest . . .[7]May God in his mercy spare her and give her a long life!

With best wishes to all,
Yours very sincerely,
C.H. Pandya

---

[5] As in the original.
[6] As in the original.
[7] As in the original.

Appendix VI

Letter from Chhaganlal Harilal Pandya to the Author[8]

Nadiad
7 August 1903

My dear Govardhanbhai,

I have gone through—with much painful interest—
the portion you have already written and, let
me acknowledge, I could not prevent tears from
spontaneously overflowing in my eyes when I came
across certain passages, episodes which I knew but
too well.

I had a very high regard for the dear deceased, but
your present effusion of heart has disclosed certain
precious traits in her character which I had not the
opportunity of being acquainted with and which
hardly anyone else but those nearest her could be
expected to be acquainted with while she was alive.

---

[8] The original letter is in English.

Such a noble self-sacrifice is indeed exemplary, and I doubt not but that the publication of this small book will benefit numerous readers who suffer more or less as she has suffered.

Your exposition of her high moral character has increased my regard for her a hundredfold, and the fear that I may not be able to control my feelings if I try to speak about her to you in person, (which) deters me from seeing you again and, therefore, I return the manuscript herewith with thanks.

Yours very sincerely,
C.H. Pandya

Appendix VII

Letter from Krishnalal Mohanlal Jhaveri to the Author[9]

Bombay,
Giragaon Post
16 January 1902

---

[9] The original letter is in English.

My Dear Govardhanbhai,

It was only today that I learnt from Bhavnagar that poor Lilavati has in spite of all your loving care succumbed to the disease. It is indeed a great blow to you. Especially when one thinks of what an ideal girl she was, one feels as if one has lost a gem from our womankind. I offer to you my sincere sympathy in this bereavement, and I consider myself particularly fortunate that I was brought in contact with such a good girl only so shortly before she left us.

Let us hope that Lalita Bhabhi would take it as forbearingly as you must be doing, and that it does not bear seriously on her health.

Yours obediently,
Krishnalal

Appendix VIII

This Author's Letter to Krishnalal Mohanlal Jhaveri[10]

My dear Krishnalal,

Your letter to me and mine to you about Lilavati have crossed each other.

You call her an 'ideal girl' and, if I differ from you in that description, it is because I know that she would have been still more 'ideal' if Providence had taught me better.

That a girl so 'ideal' should have now been reduced to a mere 'idea' of memory and that she should have suffered so much socially and in point of health, these and other ideas now haunt me and cause at times a deep-seated agony in my heart. She had inherited not only the best traits that I am conscious of having within me or within her mother, but she had more valuable additions in her own intellectual calibre and moral stamina—

---

[10] The original letter is in English.

things for which credit was due to her own soul rather than to any heredity. I do not so much feel her death as her agonies in life and death, and it is an uphill task for my philosophy to conquer my mortal feelings for one so sweet, so virtuous, and, if I am not doting, so great too. Nay, the very act that I have been able to pick up my fortitude and philosophy so far as to beat all my previous record of my hardness of heart on similar occasions in my past life, makes me shudder at myself. Her mother also, though disconsolate at times, shows an unexpected fortitude which surprises all here. I am almost inclined to be superstitious and to give credence to the idea that the stout soul now departed is extending her sacred shadow from the invisible world and screening her late parents from the frailties of bereaved world. It was the great anxiety of her life while she lived to conceal her sufferings from me, and she openly and up to the last moment severely rebuked her mother for not showing the fortitude which the philosophy, given to her and to her mother by me, ought to have enabled them to pick up. At least the child's own example in the direction serves us for a lesson, and we try to follow her wishes and her noble example in memory of her.

The usual custom of our caste would have compelled our family to keep up a system of wailing and weeping through the year. At the risk of being disapproved by some, I minimised the whole thing into a noontime mourning and weeping for the ladies for the first nine days and substituted a Katha of Upanishad[11] taught to her for the hour of evening *Bethamana*.[12] Yesterday was the day for even the last shade of her death to be over. A vision of life and death has passed away from my worldly presence; and believing as I do in one all-permeating unity of soul divine, I try to look upon her as still alive in a higher form and in a stage where He that has taken will take me too.

Yours Sincerely,
Govardhanram M. Tripathi

---

[11] Katha and Upanishad both written in Gujarati in the original English letter.

[12] 'Bethamana'—Gujarati in the original—a practice of 'seating with' the bereaved family.

Appendix IX

The letter from Krishnalal Mohanlal Jhaveri to the Author[13]

Bombay,
19 January 1902

My dear Govardhanbhai,

I am in receipt of your letter. Never, since I had the good fortune of coming in intimate contact with you, have I seen a writing so eloquent and so feeling come from your pen. The way in which you describe the deceased and the conflict of your feeling almost brought tears into my eyes. It is true that, when out of the fullness of the mind the heart speaketh, its speech is as feeling and simple as it is eloquent. When the innermost recesses of your heart are moved—and it is only excessive grief or joy which does so—involuntarily you speak a language which

---

[13] The original letter is in English.

appeals to all. Grief chastens our feelings, and, in that chastened state, one heart responds as readily to the other as things like each other are expected to do. My feeling for her and consequently my grief for losing such an exemplary soul are genuine: they yield in no way to those that are entertained by her nearest and dearest relatives and consequently it is that I find my heart also beating in unison with yours and see the struggle that has more than unmanned you. The least tribute that I can give to her memory is the wish that, if one is fated to have a daughter born to one, may she be another Lilavati!

When I was at Nadiad, I was almost tempted to tell you that it was strange to see Lilavati being the mistress of some of the best qualities of our race, which neither you nor Lalita Bhabhi possessed. But I thought I would be going far beyond the limits of my regard for you if I said so. As I now see that independently of my saying so, you too have come to the same conclusion, I have no hesitation in saying that I fully agree with you in that respect.

~

I am indeed glad that in observing these obsequies you have paid all regard you can to the favourite bent of her mind. 'Sweets to the Sweet,' says Hamlet somewhere in speaking of Ophelia. Similarly, Upanishad reading is but the fitting offering that we mortals can give to the shade of a departed and immortal soul that had all the simplicity and all the guilelessness of the saints and rishis of those far off days.

Time of course will do this work and the keenness of the blow become dull by and by; but the example she has left behind her will have its brightness, I hope, never dimmed.

Yours obediently,
Krishnalal.

Appendix X

Letter from Harsukhram Panditram Pandya to the Author[14]

Junagadh
9 January

My dear Govardhanbhai,

Extremely sorry to learn that poor Lilavati is no more. I have never seen a girl so quiet, unassuming, and virtuous. May her soul rest in eternal peace. Pray accept our sympathies and consolation.

With best regards,
Yours most sincerely,
Harsukhram

---

[14] The original letter is in English.

Appendix XI

Letter from Gopaldas Viharidas Desaiji to the Author[15]

Sihore
15 January 1902

My dear Govardhanbhai,

I was much grieved to learn that after all poor Lilavati could not be spared. The memory of her lovely disposition, virtue, and wisdom will ever remain in the hearts of those who had the privilege of knowing her. May her soul rest in peace eternal.

~

With kind regards,
I remain
Yours sincerely,
Gopaldas V.

---

[15] The original letter is in English.

Appendix XII

Letter from Janmashanker Mahashankar Buch
'Lalit' for the Author[16]

Baroda,
Ghee Kanta,
Bhutadi Zampa,
21 January 1902

~

I am much grieved to learn from Mr Ramaniyabhai
the sad and sudden death of Lilavati Bahen. The
pending death—stroke did befall, as it boded long
since. It revives the heart-rending pathos running
through the elegy of your late sister. 'It is a woe too
deep for tears.' Loving parents with all their efforts
to forget such an irony of fate cannot but feel the
reaction bitterly.

---

[16] The original letter is in English.

It is really 'passing strange and wonderful' that the budding blossoms of both the sexes of our present society, writhing under the *Sampratyatmak* system of conventional life, thus wither and fade like martyrs of *Purushayajna* before their prime and that the stern reality converts, for a while, even 'Philosophy's Accepted Guest' engulfed in deep sorrow, to regret the seeming failure of the active optimism bringing home the positive truth of the so styled Dream Land of *Siddhashram* wherein she, a sweet soul, may rest in peace 'to be an echo and a light unto Eternity' in order to guide the suffering humanity below! Amen!

Pray do convey my faltering word of condolence to my saintly and motherly Lalita Bahen.

~

I am
Yours obediently,
Janmashanker M. Buch

Appendix XIII

Letter from the Author to Janmanshanker
Mahashanker Buch[17]

Nadiad,
24 January 1902

My dear Janmanshanker,

Thanks for your kind letter about Lilavati as also for
the kind and tender sentiments which your affection
for me and mine has evoked from your pen.

My sister's memory is, no doubt, woven up in
my mind with my daughter's. They both had such
special affection and partiality for each other in life
and it seems now in death too. But there was all the
contrast that circumstances could create, between
their careers in life.

While your study of my latest book has enabled
you to describe their marraiges in my own language,

---

[17] The original letter is in English.

there was all that could be said in favour of my sister's conjugal blessedness. Her life was one of a sweet, happy and thankful association of soul with one whose elevated love and fortunate circumstances enabled him to make her hardly less happy than any couple of European love.

To my poor Lilavati, was, however, reserved an obstinately unlucky lot in which financial difficulties played no insignificant part. And with the philosophy and sweetness that her education and innate powers were able to develop in her, her life became one of martyrdom, among other things, to her own very high sense of duty, in which point she out-distanced not only me and mind but all the characters that I have been able to spin out in my books.

Hers, thus, became a life of upward spiritual *ascent by sacrifice*[18] of all worldly concerns; and if her life was so continuously one of a struggle for which her slender body proved quite unequal, she had always all that superior power and elevation of soul

---

[18] Emphasis in the original.

which is inevitably born of all deliberate sacrifice of life in good and noble causes.

Her *Purushyajna* to which you refer was of the highest type that I have met with in life and that is a mine of consolation to my soul too.

She had long since been aware of the gravity of her illness and had done her best to strengthen her poor mother's heart for the impending separation. But a mother, of course, is a mother after all.

I shall be happy to know from time to time about your own progress in life.

My best compliments to Mr Manirai (T. Joshipara BA, LLB of Junagadh, now at Baroda). I know him by name.

With best wishes,
Govardhanram M. Tripathi

PS: Ramanik goes to Bombay as there is plague here.

Appendix XIV

Letter from Kanaiyalal Jhaverilal Yajnik to the Author[19]

Bombay,
Abhyankar's Chawl
15 January 1902

Dear Sir,

It was a great pain to hear of the sad and the most untimely death of Lilavati who was not only your best child but was one whom I always regarded as the best of her sex in Nagarwada at least. I sympathise with you and your whole family in this sad bereavement, but I feel most particularly for Ben Lalita who by nature is least fitted to bear such a heart-rending blow.

Her loss to us all is irreparable and it is impossible to forget her soon or to remember her

---

[19] The original letter is in English.

except with a feeling of peculiar pain. But it ought now to be the sincere prayer of all who are bound to your family with ties of affection or relation that the misfortune—heavy as it is—may end there and be not the future cause of further misfortune. It is earnest prayer to the causer of all causes that he may give Ben Lalita, you, Ranchhodbhai and all members of your family strength enough to bear this heavy loss and misfortune with calm resignation.

I remain,
Sir,
Yours obediently,
Kanaiyalal J. Yajnik